# Our World Belongs to God

## A Contemporary Testimony

## Study Edition

FAITH
ALIVE®
Christian Resources

Grand Rapids, Michigan

Faith Alive Christian Resources published by CRC Publications
Our World Belongs to God: A Contemporary Testimony, Study Version, © 1987 by CRC Publications, 2850 Kalamazoo Ave. SE, Grand Rapids, MI 49560. All rights reserved. With the exception of brief excerpts for review purposes, no part of this book may be reproduced in any manner whatsoever without written permission from the publisher. Printed in the United States of America on recycled paper.

ISBN 0-930265-31-9

10 9 8 7 6 5 4 3

# Contents

# Using This Study Edition

You are reading a revised study edition of Our World Belongs to God: A Contemporary Testimony. This study edition contains—in addition to the final version of the Testimony itself—a Commentary on thirty-eight major topics, amplifying and applying statements made in the Testimony. Discussion questions follow each topic in the Commentary.

The Testimony and its Commentary are the work of the Contemporary Testimony Committee. The committee's work was given final approval by the Christian Reformed Synod of 1986, which also instructed CRC Publications to prepare this study edition.

While individuals may want to study this booklet at home on their own, its intended audience is small groups in the church: adult or young-adult church school classes, Bible-study groups, midweek classes, church committees, and so on. The number of times a group may meet to study this booklet is flexible. Some groups could hold up to thirty-nine meetings, one on the Introduction of this study edition (p. 7) and one on each of the thirty-eight topics of the Commentary. Others may want to meet only once or twice, taking just one or two topics from the Commentary. For example, a Bible-study group might study the material on inerrancy. A Christian school committee could discuss the Commentary's treatment of education. A youth group might be interested in what the Commentary says about the occult, earthkeeping, or human rights. An evangelism committee could examine the material on missions. A worship committee could look at the sections on the sacraments and on liturgy and worship. Regardless of the number of sessions held, a good rule of thumb is not to take more than two topics from the Commentary at any single forty-five- to sixty-minute session; in fact, a single topic for each session is often best.

Discussion groups should pattern their meetings according to their own schedules and interests. Our comments here—and our study questions—are suggestions you may or may not find helpful.

A typical group meeting might begin with a reading of the appropriate section of the Testimony and its supporting Scripture passages. The class could then read the Commentary silently or aloud; most sections are not long, and a fresh reading is helpful for discussion. Then the group could turn to the discussion questions, choosing those of greatest interest to the group or framing other questions for discussion. Groups considering further study on a topic should note that many of the Commentary sections list *Acts of Synod* references which apply to the issue under discussion. Access to a set of recent *Acts of Synod* will be helpful, as will a classroom supply of *Psalter Hymnals* (for referring to the creeds). Study sessions will be enhanced if the congregation uses the Testimony as part of its worship services.

We at CRC Publications hope this study booklet will not only acquaint groups and individuals with the Contemporary Testimony but also encourage them to voice their faith, to speak to urgent issues of the day, and to serve the Lord in our society.

The Education Department
CRC Publications

# A Contemporary Testimony
# An Introduction

## History

The movement which produced the Contemporary Testimony began around 1970. A CRC pastor had preached a series of sermons which drew heavily on the teachings of the three Reformed creeds—the Heidelberg Catechism, the Belgic Confession, and the Canons of Dort. Many in the congregation responded enthusiastically, but some noted that the confessions "don't speak very clearly" when read on their own, without pastoral explanation.

These reactions set the pastor to thinking. He wondered whether it was time to update the creeds, to restate the biblical message and the Reformed faith in a more contemporary form. The pastor brought his concerns to the church council, which eventually proposed to classis that a new confession be written. Classis endorsed the idea and sent it on to synod. This led to nearly a decade of discussion about the necessity and desirability of such a venture.

Some wondered why we needed a new confession. After all, our present creeds have served us well for almost four hundred years. Generations have profited from them. Why write a new confession?

One answer that emerged was that the world has changed a lot since our newest confession was written over three hundred fifty years ago. We have technology and nuclear weapons, communism and consumerism. We can make a phone call to Europe with the push of a button and bring every heresy and false religion into our homes with the twist of a dial. Time-tested truths need to be restated in fresh ways to function in the present world.

Another answer called attention to the many challenges we face today, challenges which the writers of the historic confessions did not and could not foresee. For example, the church and the Christian community have not been immune to the secular spirit that pervades our society. To keep silent about this secularism would betray our Lord, his Word, and the faith. We are called to speak out confessionally, guiding the church to remain truly Reformed.

During the 1970s the matter of a new confession appeared repeatedly on synod's agenda. One suggested—and rejected—approach was to replace our present confessions with a new one. The same synod that rejected that approach appointed a committee to consider whether the present confessions needed to be "augmented" by a more contemporary statement of faith. A questionnaire circulated throughout the denomination indicated that there was no agreement on this approach either. Still the idea would not die. Synods urged continued study by the congregations and by a committee on this matter.

Because writing a new confession seemed to imply dropping the older ones, eventually the emphasis shifted to writing a *contemporary testimony*, the term and concept of which had a more tentative, supplementary sound. Churches would be able to test the merits of such a contemporary testimony, modify it, and eventually determine whether it should gain the status of a confession, along with the other three classical Reformed creeds.

Under these conditions synod declared itself in favor of formulating a contemporary testimony as the church's prophetic voice in addressing the critical issues of our times. In 1983 synod approved Our World Belongs to God: A Contemporary Testimony for provisional "use in worship, education, and outreach."

Three years later, after extensive testing in the churches and subsequent revision, the Synod of 1986 gave final approval to Our World Belongs to God as "a testimony of faith for our times, subordinate to our creeds and confessions." The same synod also said that a commentary be provided as "a helpful guideline for the discussion of current issues in the church."

## FORMAT

What is the best format for a contemporary testimony? The committee had several choices. They could have simply added footnotes to our present creeds. Or they could have directly addressed a cluster of current concerns such as marriage, family, education, race, nuclear armaments, and the environment. However, such piecemeal approaches would have soon been outdated. Moreover, they would not adequately respond to the secular challenge of our times.

Therefore the Contemporary Testimony Committee decided to write the Contemporary Testimony from a single, central perspective: the biblical idea of the coming kingdom. The theme of the Testimony would be "Our World Belongs to God," and it would take on the secular claims of our day with a clear confession of God's kingdom. It would help believers give voice to their faith. It would encourage Christians to serve the Lord in society and to testify to their beliefs about current issues. It would be used in worship, in church education, and in day-to-day experience.

Because of its biblical, kingdom perspective, the Contemporary Testimony closely follows the basic story line of the biblical message. It moves from creation through the fall to redemption on the way toward renewed creation. Under each of these main headings it confesses the Christian position regarding matters of crucial concern to the Christian community today.

The Contemporary Testimony is organized into three levels. First, the *Preamble* introduces and in a few lines states the central theme, "Our World Belongs to God." As a confession, the Preamble can stand on its own. Second, the *Testimony* itself elaborates more fully and concretely the central ideas introduced in the Preamble. Both the Preamble and the Testimony are written in prose-verse form, divided into numbered stanzas for easy use and ready reference.

Third, the *Commentary* offers a deeper analysis and critique of the key issues addressed in the Testimony. Each section in the Commentary begins by quoting relevant passages from the Testimony, discusses the issues, then closes by citing, whenever possible, pertinent synodical decisions.

The Commentary is somewhat open-ended: outdated sections could be dropped and new sections added as new challenges arise. The Commentary should help groups discuss Our World Belongs to God.

It is the prayer of the Contemporary Testimony Committee that this Testimony may help you live by faith in God's world and that some of these words may assist you in giving reason for the hope that you have through our Lord Jesus Christ.

It is our joy that this complex, worrisome world belongs to God!

Contemporary Testimony Committee
G. J. Spykman, chairman     R. J. Mouw
M. N. Greidanus, reporter   B. Nederlof
R. Recker, secretary        C. Vandervelde
L. Den Besten               A. Van Ginkel
C. Hoogendoorn

DISCUSSION QUESTIONS ON THE INTRODUCTION

1.  What are several of the most formidable challenges facing us in our modern secular age? Do you feel the need for a new confession or "contemporary testimony" to address these challenges?

2.  Our present confessions reflect the age in which they were written and the issues the church faced then. Consider, for example, the attention given to the doctrine of the Lord's Supper and the questions related to merit and grace. What teachings would you emphasize if you were writing a confession for our times: the authority of Scripture? the doctrine of creation? the kingdom of God? the covenant of grace? the value of human life? the mission of the church in the world? the gifts of the Spirit? others?

3.  It took nearly a decade for the church to get this project under way. What are your reactions to such caution? In your judgment what conditions would the Contemporary Testimony have to meet to gain the status of a fourth confession? (*Note:* Confessions traditionally have three purposes: to restate the basic teachings of Scripture; to promote the church's unity; to serve as a witness in and to the world.) In your discussion you might also consider what accounts for the time-tested and enduring quality of our three Reformed creeds.

4.  For over four hundred years the Lutheran churches have lived with a single creed—the Augsburg Confession of 1530. Meanwhile Reformed churches have produced dozens of creeds. How do you account for this? What does it say about our Reformed understanding of the role of confessions?

5.  Each of our creeds has a somewhat different organization and style. How is the Contemporary Testimony different in organization and style from the other Reformed creeds? What are your general impressions of its organization and prose-verse style?

6.  Discuss how the central theme, "Our World Belongs to God," is true to Scripture and our present creeds. To what extent is the theme relevant to the secular challenges of our time?

7.  The three-level structure of the Contemporary Testimony is intended to enhance its usefulness in the life of the church, lending it a certain flexibility. How might the Testimony be used in our worship services? What might its uses be for church education? For ecumenical contacts? For missions and evangelism? For public witness?

# Confessional References

The numbers in each column refer to stanzas of the Contemporary Testimony, to questions and answers of the Heidelberg Catechism (not to Lord's Days), to articles of the Belgic Confession, and to heads and articles of the Canons of Dort.

| Stanza | Heidelberg Catechism | Belgic Confession | Canons of Dort |
|---|---|---|---|
| 1 | 1, 50 | 1 | |
| 2 | 128-129 | 2 | |
| 3 | 7-10 | | |
| 4 | 27 | | |
| 5 | | 13 | |
| 6 | 21-25; 64, 86 | | |
| 7 | 26 | 12 | |
| 8 | | 2, 8-9 | |
| 9 | 26 | | |
| 10 | 6, 124 | 14 | |
| 11 | 108 | | |
| 12 | 105-107 | | |
| 13 | 27-28 | 13 | |
| 14 | 7-11, 94-97 | 14-15 | I, 1; III-IV, 1-4 |
| 15 | 5, 8 | | |
| 16 | 96 | | |
| 17 | 3-5, 104-108 | | |
| 18 | 9-11 | | |
| 19 | 19 | 17 | I, 1-2 |
| 20 | | 17 | |
| 21 | 27 | | |
| 22 | | 25 | I, 3-4; III-IV, 5 |
| 23 | 31 | | |
| 24 | 12-20, 29-36 | 10, 18-21 | |
| 25 | 31, 37 | | |
| 26 | 16 | | |
| 27 | 37-45, 59-64 | 21-23 | II, 9 |
| 28 | 29 | 16-20, 22-23 | I, II |
| 29 | 46-51 | 26 | |
| 30 | 49, 51-53 | 11 | |
| 31 | | 24 | III, IV, V |
| 32 | | | II, 5 |
| 33 | 32, 55 | | |
| 34 | | 2-7 | |
| 35 | | 7 | |
| 36 | 19, 21-22 | | |
| 37 | | | II, 9 |
| 38 | 54 | 27-29 | |
| 39 | 116-119 | 30-32 | |
| 40 | 65-82 | 33-35 | |
| 41 | 55, 86 | | |
| 42 | 83-85, 126 | | V |

| | | | |
|---|---|---|---|
| 43 | 54 | 27-29 | |
| 44 | 123 | | II, 5; III-IV, 6 |
| 45 | 122 | | |
| 46 | 105-107 | | |
| 47 | 108-109 | | |
| 48 | 108 | | |
| 49 | 104 | 34 | I, 17 |
| 50 | | | III-IV, 17 |
| 51 | 103, 110-111, 124-125 | | |
| 52 | 107, 124 | | |
| 53 | 104, 123 | 36 | |
| 54 | 105, 112 | 36 | |
| 55 | 105-107 | | |
| 56 | 123 | | |
| 57 | 52, 57 | 37 | |
| 58 | 58 | 37 | |

# OUR WORLD BELONGS TO GOD
# A Contemporary Testimony

## PREAMBLE

1. As followers of Jesus Christ,[1]
   living in this world—
   which some seek to control,
   but which others view with despair—[2]
   we declare with joy and trust:
   Our world belongs to God![3]
   > [1] Ps. 103:19-22
   > [2] Ps. 4:6
   > [3] Ps. 24:1

2. From the beginning,[1]
   through all the crises of our times,
   until his kingdom fully comes,[2]
   God keeps covenant forever.
   Our world belongs to him![3]
   God is King! Let the earth be glad!
   Christ is Victor; his rule has begun. Hallelujah!
   The Spirit is at work, renewing the creation. Praise the Lord!
   > [1] Ps. 145
   > [2] Rom. 11:33-36
   > [3] Rev. 4-5

3. But rebel cries sound through the world:[1]
   some, crushed by failure
   or hardened by pain,
   give up on life and hope and God;
   others, shaken,
   but still hoping for human triumph,[2]
   work feverishly to realize their dreams.[3]
   As believers in God
   we join this struggle of the spirits,
   testing our times by the Spirit's sure Word.
   > [1] Ps. 2
   > [2] Eph. 6:10-18
   > [3] 1 John 4

4. Our world has fallen into sin;
   but rebellion and sin can never dethrone God.[1]
   | He does not abandon the work of his hand;
   the heavens still declare his glory.
   | He preserves his world,
   sending seasons, sun, and rain,[2]
   upholding his creatures,

renewing the earth,
directing all things to their purpose.
He promised a Savior;
now the whole creation groans[3]
in the birth pangs of a new creation.

[1] Ps. 19
[2] Acts 14:15-17
[3] Rom. 8:18-25

5.   God holds this world[1]
in sovereign love.
He kept his promise,
sending Jesus into the world.
He poured out his Spirit[2]
and broadcast the news
that sinners who repent and believe in Jesus[3]
can live
and breathe
and move again
as members of the family of God.

[1] John 3:1-21
[2] Acts 2
[3] Acts 17:22-31

6.   We rejoice in the goodness of God,
renounce the works of darkness,
and dedicate ourselves to holy living.
As covenant partners,
called to faithful obedience,[1]
and set free for joyful praise,
we offer our hearts and lives[2]
to do God's work in his world.[3]
With tempered impatience, eager to see injustice ended,
we expect the Day of the Lord.
And we are confident
that the light which shines in the present darkness[4]
will fill the earth when Christ appears.

Come, Lord Jesus![5]
Our world belongs to you.

[1] Mic. 6:8
[2] Rom. 12:1-2
[3] 2 Pet. 3
[4] 1 Cor. 15
[5] Rev. 22:20

CREATION

7.   Our world belongs to God—
     not to us or earthly powers,[1]
     not to demons, fate, or chance.
     The earth is the Lord's!
          [1] Deut. 10:12-14

8.   In the beginning, God—[1]
     Father, Word, and Spirit—[2]
     called this world into being[3]
     out of nothing,
     and gave it
     shape and order.
          [1] Gen. 1
          [2] Ps. 33:1-11
          [3] Isa. 40

9.   God formed the land, the sky, and the seas,[1]
     making the earth a fitting home
     for the plants, animals,[2]
     and humans he created.
     The world was filled with color, beauty, and variety;
     it provided room for
     work and play,
     worship and service,
     love and laughter.
     God rested—[3]
     and gave us rest.
     In the beginning
     everything was very good.
          [1] Gen. 1-2
          [2] Ps. 104 - providence
          [3] Mark 2:27-28

10.  As God's creatures we are made in his image[1]
     to represent him on earth,[2]
     and to live in loving communion with him.
     By sovereign appointment we are[3]
     earthkeepers and caretakers:
     loving our neighbor,
     tending the creation,
     and meeting our needs.
     God uses our skills
     in the unfolding and well-being of his world.
          [1] Gen. 1:26-30
          [2] Ps. 8
          [3] Matt. 22:35-40

11. Male and female,[1]
    all of us are to represent God[2]
    as we do our tasks.
    Whether single or married,
    we are called to live within God's order[3]
    in lives of loving service.
    > [1] Gen. 1:26-28
    > [2] Gal. 3:26-28
    > [3] 1 Cor. 7

12. No matter what our age, or race, or color,[1]
    we are the human family together,
    for the Creator made us all.
    Since life is his gift,
    we foster the well-being of others,[2]
    protecting the unborn and helpless from harm[3]
    > [1] Acts 17:22-31
    > [2] Ps. 139
    > [3] Lev. 19; 25:35-38

13. God directs and bends to his will[1]
    all that happens in his world.
    As history unfolds in ways we only know in part,[2]
    all things—
    from crops to grades,
    from jobs to laws—
    are under his control.
    God is present in our world
    by his Word and Spirit.
    The faithfulness[3]
    of our great Provider
    gives sense to our days
    and hope to our years.
    The future is secure,
    for our world belongs to God.
    > [1] Matt. 6:25-34
    > [2] Ps. 147, 148
    > [3] Ps. 111

## THE FALL

14. Early in human history
    our first parents listened to the intruder's voice.[1]
    Rather than living by the Creator's
    word of life,
    they fell for Satan's lie
    and sinned!

They forgot their place;
they tried to be like God.
But as sinners they feared
the nearness of God
and hid from him.
[1] Gen. 3

15. Apart from grace[1]
we prove each day
that we are guilty sinners.
Fallen in that first sin,
we fail to thank God,
we break his laws,
we ignore our tasks.
Looking for life without God, we find only death;
grasping for freedom outside his law,[2]
we trap ourselves in Satan's snares;
pursuing pleasure, we lose the gift of joy.
[1] Rom. 1:18-3:23; 5:12
[2] 1 John 1:8-10

16. When humans no longer show God's image,[1]
all creation suffers.
We abuse the creation or idolize it.[2]
We are estranged from our Creator,
from our neighbor, and from all that God has made.
[1] Rom. 1
[2] Eph. 4:17-19

17. All spheres of life—[1]
marriage and family,
work and worship,
school and state,
our play and art—
bear the wounds of our rebellion.[2]
Sin is present everywhere—[3]
in pride of race,
in arrogance of nations,
in abuse of the weak and helpless,
in disregard for water, air, and soil,
in destruction of living creatures,
in slavery, deceit, terror, and war,[4]
in worship of false gods,
and frantic escape from reality.[5]
We have become victims of our own sin.
[1] Rom. 1
[2] Ps. 14
[3] Amos 1-2
[4] Jer. 17:9
[5] Isa. 28:7-8

18. In all our strivings[1]
    to excuse
    or save ourselves,
    we stand condemned[2]
    before the God of Truth.
    But our world,
    broken and scarred,[3]
    still belongs to God.
    He holds it together[4]
    and gives us hope.

    [1] Ps. 89
    [2] Rom. 1:18
    [3] Jer. 14
    [4] Rom. 5:2-5; 15:13

## REDEMPTION

19. While justly angry[1]
    God did not turn his back
    on a world bent on destruction;
    he turned his face to it in love.[2]
    With patience and tender care he set out[3]
    on the long road of redemption
    to reclaim the lost as his people[4]
    and the world as his kingdom.

    [1] Gen. 3:9-15
    [2] John 3:16
    [3] Luke 1:68-75; 3:23-37
    [4] Rev. 11:15

*God's active plan of redemption; remnants of those who followed him were spared from judgment*

20. Although Adam and Eve were expelled from the garden[1]
    and their work was burdened by sin's effects,
    God held on to them in love.
    He promised to crush
    the evil forces they unleashed.

    [1] Gen. 3:15-19

21. When evil filled the earth,[1]
    God judged it with a flood,
    but rescued Noah and his family[2]
    and animals of all kinds.
    He covenanted with every creature
    that seasons would continue
    and that such destruction would not come again
    until the final day.

    [1] Gen. 6-9
    [2] 1 Pet. 3:18-22

22. The Creator pledged to be God[1]
to Abraham and his children,
blessing all nations through them
as they lived obediently before him.
He chose Israel as his special people[2]
to show the glory of his name,[3]
the power of his love,[4]
and the wisdom of his ways.
He gave them his laws through Moses[5]
he led them by rulers and teachers,
so that they would be a people
whose God was king.

> [1] Gen. 12:1-3
> [2] Deut. 7
> [3] Rom. 9
> [4] Mic. 6:8
> [5] Ps. 103:7

23. When Israel spurned God's love[1]
by lusting after other gods,
by trusting in power and wealth,
and by hurting the weak,
God scattered his people among the nations.
Yet he kept a faithful few[2]
and promised them the Messiah:
a prophet to speak the clear word,
a king to crush the serpent's head,
a priestly servant willing to be broken for sinners.[3]
And he promised the gift of the Spirit[4]
to bend stubborn wills to new obedience.

> [1] 2 Chron. 36
> [2] Isa. 10
> [3] Isa. 53
> [4] Jer. 11; 31

*Christ*

24. God remembered his promise[1]
to reconcile the world to himself;
he has come among us[2]
in Jesus Christ,
the eternal Word made flesh.[3]
He is the long-awaited Savior,[4]
fully human and fully divine,
conceived by the Spirit of God
and born of the virgin Mary.

> [1] 2 Cor. 5:18-21
> [2] Gal. 4:4-7
> [3] John 1:1-14
> [4] Luke 1-2

25. In the events of his earthly life—[1]
his temptations and suffering,[2]
his teaching and miracles,
his battles with demons and talks with sinners—
Jesus made present in deed and in word
the coming rule of God.
> [1] Luke 4
> [2] Phil. 2:1-11

26. As the second Adam he chose[1]
the path we had rejected.
As our representative,
serving God perfectly,
and loving even those who scorned him,[2]
Christ showed us how
a righteous child of God lives.
> [1] Rom. 5
> [2] 1 Pet. 2:21-25

27. As our substitute[1]
he suffered all his years on earth,
especially in the horrible torture of the cross.
He carried God's judgment on our sin;[2]
his sacrifice removes our guilt.
He walked out of the grave, the Lord of life!
He conquered sin and death.[3]
We are set right with God,
we are given new life,
and called to walk with him[4]
in freedom from sin's dominion.
> [1] Isa. 53
> [2] Heb. 10
> [3] Rom. 4:18-5:11
> [4] Gal. 5

28. Being both God and man,[1]
Jesus is the only Mediator    See # 24
between God and his people.
He alone paid the debt of our sin;[2]
there is no other Savior!
In him the Father chose those[3]
whom he would save.
His electing love sustains our hope:
God's grace is free
to save sinners who offer nothing
but their need for mercy.
> [1] 1 Tim. 2:5-6
> [2] Acts 4:10-12
> [3] Eph. 1:1-14

HC 29

29.  Jesus ascended in triumph[1]
     to his heavenly throne.[2]
     There he hears our prayers,
     pleads our cause before the Father,[3]
     and rules the world.[4]
     Blessed are all[5]
     who take refuge in him.
     > [1] Acts 1:1-11
     > [2] Eph. 1:18-23
     > [3] 1 John 2:1-2
     > [4] Rev. 5
     > [5] Rom. 8:31-39

*Mediatorial work of X*

*The Spirit* – *work of the Spirit*

30.  At Pentecost the Holy Spirit[1]
     was given to the church.
     In pouring his Spirit on many peoples
     God overcomes the divisions of Babel;[2]
     now people from every tongue, tribe, and nation
     are gathered into the unity
     of the body of Christ.
     > [1] Acts 2
     > [2] Rev. 7

*In Church*

31.  Jesus stays with us in the Spirit,[1]
     who renews our hearts,
     moves us to faith,
     leads us in the truth,[2]
     stands by us in our need,
     and makes our obedience fresh and vibrant.
     > [1] John 14
     > [2] 2 Cor. 3:7-18

*In us*

32.  The Spirit thrusts[1]
     God's people into worldwide mission.
     He impels young and old,[2]
     men and women,
     to go next door and far away[3]
     into science and art,
     media and marketplace
     with the good news of God's grace.
     The Spirit goes before them and with them,[4]
     convincing the world of sin
     and pleading the cause of Christ.
     > [1] Matt. 28:18-20
     > [2] Matt. 9:35-38
     > [3] Luke 14:15-24
     > [4] John 16:5-15

*3 charge given to everyone*

*Kuyperian*

33. The Spirit's gifts are here to stay[1]
    in rich variety—
    fitting responses to timely needs.
    We thankfully see each other
    as gifted members of the fellowship[2]
    which delights in the creative Spirit's work.
    He gives more than enough
    to each believer
    for God's praise and our neighbor's welfare.[3]

    [1] 1 Cor. 12-14
    [2] Eph. 4
    [3] Rom. 12

*Scripture*

34. God has not left this world[1]
    without ways of knowing him.
    He shows his power and majesty
    in the creation;    — *nature*
    he has mercifully spoken
    through prophets, history writers, poets,[2]
    gospel writers, and apostles—    — *Scripture*
    and most clearly through the Son.
    The Spirit who moved humans[3]
    to write the Word of God[4]
    speaks to us in the Bible.

    *Kuyperian?*
    *Common grace*

    [1] Rom. 1
    [2] Heb. 1
    [3] 2 Tim. 3:14-17
    [4] 2 Pet. 1:12-21

35. The Bible is the Word of God,
    record and tool of his redeeming work.
    It is the Word of Truth,[1]
    fully reliable in leading us[2]
    to know God
    and have life[3]
    in Jesus Christ.

    *Authority of Scripture*

    [1] James 1:18
    [2] Acts 8:26-39
    [3] John 20:30-31

36. The Bible tells God's mighty acts[1]
    in the unfolding of covenant history.[2]
    It is one revelation in two Testaments,
    which shows a single plan of salvation,
    and reveals God's will infallibly.

    *not dispensa-tions*

As God's people hear the Word and do it,[3]
they are equipped for discipleship,
to witness to the good news:
Our world belongs to God
and he loves it deeply.

[1] Acts 7
[2] 1 Cor. 10:1-11
[3] 2 Tim. 3:14-17

*God's New People*[1]

[1] Eph. 1-4

37. In our world, bent under the weight of sin,
Christ gathers a new community.[1]
Satan and his evil forces
seek whom they may confuse and swallow;[2]
but Jesus builds his church,[3]
his Spirit guides,
and grace abounds.

[1] 1 Pet. 5:8-11
[2] 1 Cor. 3:10-17
[3] Matt. 16:13-19

38. The church is the fellowship of those[1]
who confess Jesus as Lord.
She is the Bride of Christ,
his chosen partner,[2]
loved by Jesus and loving him:[3]
delighting in his presence,
seeking him in prayer,[4]
silent before the mystery of his love.

[1] Rev. 21:9
[2] 1 Pet. 2:4-10
[3] Eph. 2
[4] Col. 1:1-23; 3:1-17

39. Our new life in Christ[1]
is celebrated and nourished
in the fellowship of congregations[2]
where God's name is praised,
his Word proclaimed,[3]
his way taught;
where sins are confessed,[4]
prayers and gifts are offered,[5]
and sacraments are celebrated.

[1] Acts 2:41-47
[2] Eph. 4:1-5:20
[3] Rom. 10
[4] Eph. 3:1-13
[5] Matt. 6:5-15

40.  God meets us in the sacraments,[1]
holy acts in which his deeds[2]
elicit our response.
God reminds and assures us in baptism,[3]
whether of those newly born or newly converted,[4]
that his covenant love saves us,
that he washes away our guilt,[5]
gives us the Spirit,
and expects our love in return.
In the supper our Lord offers[6]
the bread and cup to believers
to guarantee our share
in his death and resurrection,
and to unite us to him[7]
and to each other.
We take this food gladly,[8]
announcing as we eat
that Jesus is our life
and that he shall come again[9]
to call us to the Supper of the Lamb.

> [1] Gen. 17
> [2] Ex. 12
> [3] Matt. 28:18-20
> [4] Acts 2:37-41
> [5] Col. 2:9-14
> [6] Matt. 26:26-29
> [7] 1 Cor. 10:16-17
> [8] 1 Cor. 11:17-34
> [9] Rev. 19:6-9

*universal Church*

41.  The Spirit empowers each member[1]
to take part in the ministry of all,
so that hurts are healed
and all may rejoice[2]
in the life and growth of the fellowship.

> [1] 1 Cor. 12-13
> [2] 1 Cor. 1:1-9

42.  The church is a gathering[1]
of forgiven sinners,
called to be holy,[2]
dedicated to service.
Saved by the patient grace of God,[3]
we deal patiently with others.
Knowing our own weakness and failures,
we bring good news to all sinners
with understanding of their condition,
and with hope in God.

> [1] Eph. 2
> [2] 1 Pet. 1
> [3] Matt. 5:43-48

43. We grieve that the church[1]
    which shares one Spirit, one faith, one hope,
    and spans all time, place, race, and language[2]
    has become a broken communion in a broken world.
    When we struggle for the purity of the church
    and for the righteousness God demands,
    we pray for saintly courage.
    When our pride or blindness blocks
    the unity of God's household,
    we seek forgiveness.
    We marvel that the Lord gathers the broken pieces[3]
    to do his work,
    and that he blesses us still
    with joy, new members,
    and surprising evidences of unity.
    We commit ourselves to seeking and expressing
    the oneness of all who follow Jesus.

    [1] Eph. 4
    [2] Gal. 3:26-29
    [3] John 17

*The Mission of God's People*

44. Following the apostles, the church is sent—[1]
    sent with the gospel of the kingdom[2]
    to make disciples of all nations,
    to feed the hungry,[3]
    and to proclaim the assurance that in the name of Christ[4]
    there is forgiveness of sin and new life
    for all who repent and believe—
    to tell the news that our world belongs to God.
    In a world estranged from God,
    where millions face confusing choices,
    this mission is central to our being,[5]
    for we announce the one name that saves.
    We repent of leaving this work to a few,
    we pray for brothers and sisters
    who suffer for the faith,
    and we rejoice that the Spirit[6]
    is waking us to see
    our mission in God's world.

    [1] Matt. 28:18-20
    [2] John 20:21-23
    [3] 1 John 3:11-24
    [4] 2 Cor. 5:11-6:2
    [5] Acts 1:8
    [6] 1 Thess. 1

45. The rule of Jesus Christ covers the whole world.[1]
    | To follow this Lord is
    | to serve him everywhere,[2]
     without fitting in,
      as light in the darkness,[3]
    | as salt in a spoiling world.
        [1] Phil. 2:1-10; 4:8-9
        [2] Rom. 12
        [3] Matt. 5:13-16

46. We serve Christ by thankfully receiving our life[1]
    as a gift from his hand.
    We protest and resist
    all abuse and harm of this gift[2]
    by abortion, pollution, gluttony,
    addiction, and all foolish risks.
        [1] 1 Cor. 6:19-20
        [2] Ps. 139

*reflects Contemporary Issues*

47. Since God made us male and female in his image,[1]
    one sex may not look down on the other,
    | nor should we flaunt or exploit our sexuality.
    | Our roles as men and women must conform[2]
    to God's gifts and commands[3]
    as we shape our cultural patterns.
    Sexuality is disordered in our fallen world;[4]
    grief and loneliness are the result;[5]
    but Christ's renewing work gives hope
    for order and healing
    and surrounds suffering persons[6]
    with a compassionate community.
        [1] Gen. 1:26-2:25
        [2] Song of Songs
        [3] Gal. 3:28
        [4] Prov. 7
        [5] 1 Cor. 6:9-20
        [6] John 8:1-11

48. We serve Christ as singles,[1]
    whether for a time or a life,
    by undivided devotion to the work of God
    and so add our love and service
    to the building of his kingdom.
        [1] 1 Cor. 7:25-35

<!-- margin note: Missions! Contemporary Issues: domestic life -->

49. In marriage and family,[1]
we serve God
by reflecting his covenant love
in life-long loyalty,
and by teaching his ways,
so that children may know Jesus as their Lord
and learn to use their gifts in a life of joyful service.
[1] Eph. 5:1-6:4

<!-- margin note: gratitude -->

<!-- margin note: Contemporary Issues: in Society - Christian schools -->

50. In education we seek to acknowledge the Lord[1]
by promoting schools and teaching[2]
in which the light of his Word shines in all learning,[3]
where students, of whatever ability,
are treated as persons who bear God's image[4]
and have a place in his plan.
[1] Prov. 4; 9:10
[2] Ps. 119:105
[3] Col. 1:17
[4] Deut. 6:1-9

51. In our work, even in dull routine,[1]
we hear the call to serve our Lord.
We must work for more than wages,[2]
and manage for more than profit,[3]
so that mutual respect
and the just use of goods and skills[4]
may shape the work place,
and so that, while we earn or profit,
useful products and services may result.
Rest and leisure are gifts of God[5]
to relax us and to set us free
to discover and to explore.
Believing that he provides for us,
we can rest more trustingly[6]
and entertain ourselves more simply.
[1] Eph. 4:17-32
[2] 2 Thess. 3:6-13
[3] Eph. 6:5-9
[4] 1 Thess. 4:9-12
[5] Phil. 4:8
[6] Heb. 4:1-13

52. Grateful for the advances
    in science and technology,[1]
    we make careful use of their products,[2]
    on guard against idolatry
    and harmful research,
    and careful to use them in ways that answer[3]
    to God's demands
    to love our neighbor
    and to care for the earth and its creatures.[4]
    > [1] Gen. 1:28-31; 9:1-7
    > [2] 1 Chron. 29:1-19
    > [3] 1 Tim. 4:1-5
    > [4] Rom. 8:19-23

53. Since God establishes the powers that rule,[1]
    we are called to respect them,[2]
    unless they trample his Word.
    We are to obey God in politics,[3]
    pray for our rulers,
    and help governments to know his will for public life.
    Knowing that God's people
    live under many forms of government,
    we are thankful for the freedoms[4]
    enjoyed by citizens of many lands;
    we grieve with those who live under oppression,[5]
    and we work for their liberty[6]
    to live without fear.
    > [1] John 19:11
    > [2] Rom. 13:1-7
    > [3] Acts 4
    > [4] Isa. 61:1-2
    > [5] Gen. 18
    > [6] Rom 6:16-19

54. We call on governments to do public justice[1]
    and to protect the freedoms and rights[2]
    of individuals, groups, and institutions,[3]
    so that each may freely do[4]
    the tasks God gives.
    We urge governments to ensure the well-being of all citizens[5]
    by protecting children from abuse and pornography,[6]
    by guarding the elderly and poor,[7]
    and by promoting the freedom to speak, to work,[8]
    to worship, and to associate.
    > [1] Matt. 5:6
    > [2] Isa. 61:8
    > [3] Luke 4:17-21
    > [4] 1 Tim. 2:1-4
    > [5] Ps. 72
    > [6] Isa. 1:16-17
    > [7] Lev. 19:13-16
    > [8] Jer. 9:23-24; 22:15-17

55. Following the Prince of Peace,[1]
    we are called to be peacemakers,
    and to promote harmony and order.
    We call on our governments to work for peace;[2]
    we deplore the arms race[3]
    and the horrors that we risk.
    We call on all nations to limit their weapons
    to those needed in the defense of justice and freedom.
    We pledge to walk in ways of peace,[4]
    confessing that our world belongs to God;
    he is our sure defense.

> [1] James 3:18
> [2] Mic. 4:1-5
> [3] Matt. 26:52
> [4] Matt. 5:9

## NEW CREATION

56. Our hope for a new earth is not tied[1]
    to what humans can do,[2]
    for we believe that one day[3]
    every challenge to God's rule
    and every resistance to his will shall be crushed.
    Then his kingdom shall come fully,[4]
    and our Lord shall rule forever.

> [1] 1 Pet. 1:3-12
> [2] 2 Pet. 3:1-13
> [3] 1 Thess. 4:13-5:11
> [4] Rev. 11:15

57. We long for that day[1]
    when Jesus will return as triumphant king,
    when the dead will be raised[2]
    and all people will stand before his judgment.[3]
    We face that day without fear,
    for the Judge is our Savior.
    Our daily lives of service aim for the moment[4]
    when the Son will present his people to the Father.
    Then God will be shown to be true, holy, and gracious.
    All who have been on the Lord's side[5]
    will be honored,
    the fruit of even small acts of[6]
    obedience will be displayed;
    but tyrants and oppressors,
    heretics, and all who deny the Lord
    will be damned.

> [1] Rev. 20:11-21:8
> [2] 1 Cor. 15
> [3] John 5:28-29
> [4] 2 Thess. 1:5-10
> [5] 2 Cor. 5:10
> [6] Matt. 25:31-46

58. With the whole creation[1]
    we wait for the purifying fire of judgment.
    For then we will see the Lord face to face.[2]
    He will heal our hurts,
    end our wars,
    and make the crooked straight.
    Then we will join in the new song
    to the Lamb without blemish[3]
    who made us a kingdom and priests.[4]
    God will be all in all,
    righteousness and peace will flourish,[5]
    everything will be made new,
    and every eye will see at last
    that our world belongs to God!
    Hallelujah! Come, Lord Jesus.[6]

[1] Rom. 8:18-39
[2] Rev. 21-22
[3] Rev. 5
[4] 1 Cor. 15:28
[5] Isa. 11:6-9; 60:11, 19-20; 65:17-25
[6] Rev. 22:17, 20

# COMMENTARY ON CONTEMPORARY ISSUES

*Note:* The Commentary is intended not so much for confessing the Christian faith as for exploring its implications. Accordingly it is open-ended; in time, outdated sections can be dropped and other sections added as new challenges arise. Each section in the Commentary opens with relevant passages from the Contemporary Testimony, discusses pertinent societal issues, then closes by citing, whenever possible, synodical decisions which bear upon the issue at hand. Discussion questions are also included.

Topics in this Commentary are arranged in order of their treatment in the Testimony.

## INTRODUCTION: THE SPIRIT OF OUR TIMES

As followers of Jesus Christ,
living in this world—
which some seek to control,
but which others view with despair—
we declare with joy and trust:
Our world belongs to God!

(Contemporary Testimony, 1)

The dominant spirit of our times has various names, such as secularism, atheism, humanism, or practical atheism. Together these forces form a real, culturally formative power which restricts and opposes God's people as they try to live obediently in this world.

If it takes a crisis to move the church to write confessional statements, these secular spirits of our times have moved us to write this Contemporary Testimony. For the impact of these spiritual powers is directly opposed to the theme "Our World Belongs to God." Atheists, secularists, and humanists think and act on the belief that this world is humanity's to save or destroy. They act as if God did not make the world and has nothing to say to it.

Secularism and humanism are really false religions in the sense that they "worship and serve the creature rather than the Creator" (Rom. 1:25). The result of both is a way of life in which God is not honored or needed: practical atheism.

Secularism is a heresy with a Christian past. It correctly rejects the pagan belief that the world is divine. However, it goes on to ignore the world's connections with God. Secularism limits humanity to this world; there are no goals, values, or truths except those which humans discover within it. Such total devotion to this world absorbs the religious fervor of millions today. Secularism is idolatry of the creation.

Humanism is also a heresy with Christian roots. It picks up the Bible's teaching on human dignity and worth, but distorts it by cutting human beings off from God, who gives them their place. The Humanist Manifesto states, "Religious humanism considers the complete realization of human personality to be the end of man's life and seeks its development and fulfillment in the here and now. . . . Man is at last becoming aware that he alone is responsible for the realization of the world of his dreams, and that he has within himself the power for its achievement" (*Humanist Manifesto I, II,* 1933, 1973).

While some atheism was known earlier (Ps. 14), it has grown as a modern development since the rise of science. Its followers proclaim that a person has come of age when he lives not by faith but by autonomous human reason. Since God cannot be discovered scientifically, they conclude that he does not count.

Such professed atheism is not that widespread. But practical atheism is! It affects everyone in our modern world. As the result of secular humanism, it tempts each citizen of this world to live as though God does not exist—without actually denying his reality. Practical atheism is the contemporary lifestyle; it shapes policies and practices in most spheres of life: government, education, business, industry, media, the arts. People are out to save and renew the world without any reference to God. The slogans are familiar: "Religion and business don't mix," "Education must be neutral," "Religion is private; public life is secular."

Because secularism and humanism have a Christian past and arose within our Western culture, they can infiltrate the life of the Christian community rather easily. Therefore, Christians are warned to "test the spirits" today too (1 John 4:1). Christians who find themselves adapting to the secular humanism of our day are called to repentance, renewal, and reformation, so that they may not be deluded by modern heresy.

In this modern crisis of a world that ignores its Maker, we testify that our world belongs to God. We point to the totality of a Christian's life in this world, for the Lord calls us to follow him everywhere. We pray that these efforts may help the church to live a vigorous Christian life and to witness daily.

1. In what ways have secularism and humanism had a "Christian past," as the Commentary asserts?

2. Give some examples of how practical atheism, secularism, or humanism has infiltrated the life of the Christian community. Consider our church life, our family life, our schools, our occupations. Do you think the forces of atheism, secularism, and humanism cause enough of a "crisis" to warrant the writing of new confessional statements? Practically speaking, how can reforming Christians respond to these challenges?

## EVOLUTIONISM

In the beginning, God—
Father, Word, and Spirit—
called this world into being
out of nothing,
and gave it
shape and order.

(Contemporary Testimony, 8)

The confession that this world belongs to God is opposed by the worldview of evolutionism. Whereas the church has agreed with Christian scholars and scientists that development takes place within the created order, evolutionism teaches the independence and autonomy of natural forces and either denies the existence of God or gives him a limited role in beginning these natural forces.

The church rejects such evolutionistic thought, which claims that this world has come about by chance or by some internal mechanism of natural selection. The allied position of social determinism is also rejected, with its view that human beings are trapped in a natural order within which they must work out their own destiny. Such a view can lead to elitism and to violence against weaker or poorer neighbors. Similar patterns of normlessness and autonomy are seen in contemporary scientific enterprises and utopian schemes. Human beings are not mere products of a naturalistic evolutionary process which moves from lower to higher forms of life, and their ethics are to be more than a survival of the fittest with its high cost in violence to other creatures.

The church rejects too the understanding of history as a development of natural progress. History is rather, from the fall of Adam and Eve, a radical struggle between the kingdom of God and the forces of evil. God's will for life has been resisted. Humans know the truth, but they suppress it in unrighteousness (Rom. 1:18). Although human rebellion has not thwarted the unfolding of the rich possibilities of the creation, the church believes that the present struggle between sin and grace will be ended not by the moral improvement of humans but by the victorious return of Jesus Christ, who will make all things new. The church is convinced that the hope of evolutionism is an illusion.

Christians are grateful for the work of all scholars whose work brings understanding of the world. They do not need to be afraid to revise previous formulations or understandings of God's dealings with this world or of the manner in which God unlocks the wealth of his created order, for the church's unshakable trust is in God, who remains the one Lord over all created reality.

Since the fact of the creation is clearly proclaimed in the Bible, we, as the church of Jesus Christ, are undaunted by the many questions of "how" and "when" that remain, which humans cannot answer with finality, and which the Bible—not being a scientific textbook—does not answer. But we believe without doubt that God willed and acted in the beginning, that the earth came into being by his sovereign design and is still kept together by his power (Gen. 1:1; Col. 1:17). All things have come into being by his active will, and all the events of history are under his control. Human beings are his covenant partners, the choice creation of the Father's, made in his image and likeness. From our Father and Creator we receive our place in the world, our task, our direction, and our hope.

On this pivotal issue of creation or evolution we trust the clear testimony of Scripture—"Our help is in the name of the Lord, the Maker of heaven and earth" (Ps 124:8). Therefore we seek to live in this world as the Father's world, delighting in what he has made, seeing his power and deity in it (Rom. 1:20). And we call on Christians in all walks of life, and on all who wish to live with meaning and hope, to renew their obedience to the authority of the Creator and his Word.

(Previous synodical statements: Creation and evolution, *Acts of Synod 1959,* pp. 81, 247-64; Origins, *Acts of Synod 1967,* pp. 76, 335-38; Genesis 1-3, *Acts of Synod 1982,* pp. 107-8.)

3.  Evolutionism is still another "spiritual power" of our age which denies, implicitly if not explicitly, that our world belongs to God. Its themes of "natural progress," "survival of the fittest," and "human beings are getting better all the time" have profoundly influenced our economic and social life.

Yet the theory of evolution does raise some difficult and challenging questions. In what specific ways have Christians revised their views of science over the last centuries? Their views of the Bible?

4. What is meant by "theistic evolution"? Should it be condemned as heresy?

## HUMAN RIGHTS

As God's creatures we are made in his image
to represent him on earth,
and to live in loving communion with him.

(Contemporary Testimony, 10)

We call on governments to do public justice
and to protect the freedoms and rights
of individuals, groups, and institutions,
so that each may freely do
the tasks God gives.

(Contemporary Testimony, 54)

Some people do not have the opportunity for work and schooling that other citizens take for granted. Such denials of opportunity are often based on racial, religious, or economic discrimination. Discrimination leads to a denial of civil liberties and oppression. In parts of the world, such as Russia and Latin America, oppression is blatant, while in other places, such as Europe and North America, it may be more subtle. But inequality in liberty and opportunity is widespread.

We are grateful for the freedoms and rights we enjoy and for efforts to end injustice and discrimination in our countries and in other parts of the world. We regret that much work for human rights is based on secular and humanist ideals, which produce rights without responsibility and frivolous applications which discredit this important cause.

The rights of people to live without oppression and discrimination because of different beliefs, lifestyles, economic status, race, or sex, or because of physical or mental disabilities are rooted in the fact that humans share the dignity of being made in the image of God. All human rights are related to people's responsibilities to deal justly with their neighbors, to protect the weak, and to allow all to fulfill their tasks in God's world.

In Christ God acted to liberate humanity from oppression in all its forms. And he gives rulers and governments the duties to act justly and to protect the welfare of citizens (Ps. 72:1-14; Luke 4:18; Rom. 13:1-7). Human rights then are based on each person's creation in God's image and on the liberating concern for the neighbor restored by Christ's redemption.

We therefore urge all citizens to respect the rights and place of the neighbors with whom they live and work.

We encourage church members to be alert to discrimination and oppression and to work for equality and justice within the institutions to which they belong.

And we call upon our various levels of government to prevent misuses of rights, to judge competing claims to rights, to protect the oppressed, and to oppose discrimination.

(Previous synodical statements: "Declarations on Race," *Acts of Synod 1968,* pp. 17ff.; "Declarations on World Hunger," *Acts of Synod 1978,* pp. 79-86.)

5.  The understanding of human rights expressed here is based on a belief that each person is created in God's image and is responsible to fulfill certain tasks in God's world. Therefore, governments are called to respect inherent human dignity and make it possible for people obediently to fulfill their tasks. Compare this view of human rights with the predominant secular view, based on "natural law" and freedom from oppression. The best one can hope for from that view is equality before law; the worst is freedom for freedom's sake. What is deficient about such notions? How could they distort the role of modern governments?

6.  The Commentary encourages church members to "work toward equality and justice within the institutions to which they belong." How, specifically, could we do this? Draw on your experience to give a practical example.

## PRAYER

As God's creatures we are made in his image
to represent him on earth,
and to live in loving communion with him.

(Contemporary Testimony, 10)

The church is the fellowship of those
who confess Jesus as Lord.
She is the Bride of Christ,
his chosen partner,
loved by Jesus and loving him:
delighting in his presence,
seeking him in prayer,
silent before the mystery of his love.

(Contemporary Testimony, 38)

The most powerful antidote to secularity is prayer. Against the denial and defiance of God that marks our time, prayer is the practice of his presence. Prayer testifies to the ultimate impossibility of a world without God (secular). To fold one's hands in prayer is to confess that God holds us and his world in his hands.

A life of true prayer faces several problems in our time. First, prayer can degenerate into an attempt to manipulate God. His promises are turned into blank checks. We fill in the amount; God only needs to sign. God is placed in a box that we have made. Second, prayer is reduced to our conscious submission to God's set plan. The only real petition left is "Thy will be done"—and it will be done, no matter what we pray. Here humans are put in a box that God is thought to have made. Third, prayer is reduced to a monologue. God is said to be bound to a cause-and-effect universe or to be part of it. Either prayer makes no sense, then, for God does not "interfere" with the world, or prayer (as conversation with God) ends, for there is no longer a conversational partner distinct from the world. Here God and the world are placed in separate boxes or enclosed in the same box. The only reason for prayer, then, is its therapeutic effect in organizing the mind.

These problems that box prayer in must be blown apart by a greater awareness that human life is covenant fellowship with God. While God remains sovereign in this fellowship, he takes us seriously. We are not robots or puppets, but his responsible representatives on earth.

Therefore, our prayers play a vital role in the drama of redemption. God promises to act in answer to prayer (Jer. 33:3; Ps. 145:18). When God lets Abraham, Moses, or Elijah in on his plans (Gen. 18; Ex. 32; 1 Kings 18), he does not evoke resignation, but earnest prayer. At times the plan unfolds as announced. At other times (Moses, Nineveh) God "repents of the evil he thought to do." God responds to prayer.

When Jesus Christ fulfills the promise of salvation, prayer gains an even larger place in the Christian life. By example and word he teaches his disciples to pray. He opens the way to God. Sinners may by grace enter God's presence (Rom. 5:2; Heb. 4:14-16). He gives the Spirit, who helps us to pray when we are weak or at a loss for words. Prayer does not depend on our boldness or eloquence, for the Spirit and the ascended Son speak to the Father for us (Rom. 8:26, 34; Heb. 7:25).

Jesus attaches astounding promises to prayer. He promises that he will do whatever we ask in his name (John 14:13; Matt. 7:7-11). These promises are so sweeping that, in a different way than secularism, they can lead to a crisis of prayer: the problem of "unanswered prayer." Studying this problem may not resolve our questions, but it can deepen our understanding of prayer.

"Unanswered" prayer becomes a problem when prayer is understood mainly as petition, and when petition is severed from the gospel of the kingdom. Prayer is "the chief part of thankfulness," and thanksgiving is to be the main part of prayer (Heidelberg Catechism, Lord's Day 45; Phil. 4:6; Col. 1:3; 2:7). In addition to thanksgiving and petition, prayer includes confession and adoration (Matt. 6:9-13; 1 Tim. 2:1-2). At first the reminder that there are other elements in prayer may not seem to help a person agonizing over unanswered prayer. But when the inner connection of the elements is seen, they have an expanding effect on each other.

In the Lord's Prayer Jesus begins by honoring God's name. This expands the next petition to include the coming kingdom. When we are focused on the kingdom, the ordinary needs for bread and forgiveness are also included. But our prayers, like those of Abraham, Elijah, and the Lord, will then also intercede for God's people and for a secular world that does not pray for itself.

Our confession of sins will do more than ask to be let off the hook; we will ask to be renewed in the ways of the kingdom. Prayer finds its place then in lives that are more and more directed by the King and toward his kingdom.

There is a link between God's answer to prayer and our obedience to his commandments (1 John 3:22-23). But this may not reduce prayer to just asking for what we have coming. For the commandment is to believe Jesus and to love each other. Following the Lord, whose prayer to let the cup pass seems unanswered, keeps us from manipulating God. And loving our neighbor as we pray will shape what we ask. Thus, in faith and love, we do not manipulate God or simply resign ourselves. We talk our needs over with God, we expect great things from him, and we trust that he knows the deepest needs of his people and the world.

There remain, of course, situations that cry out for a clear response from God . . . and it does not come! Instead we may hear, "My grace is sufficient" (2 Cor. 12:9). In these situations it may take a lifetime to learn that God's grace is not a poor second, but is more than enough.

Why do we still pray, then? Because God has taught and commanded us to pray, and because as part of our loving communion we want to talk with him. In prayer we open ourselves consciously to God's presence; we focus our lives on him. We talk to God, we listen to God, and we are silent before him, attentive to his presence. As we grow in covenant communion, we learn to pray with Augustine: "Grant me yourself, because without you my desire would not be stilled—even if I received everything you have made."

(Previous synodical statements: *Acts of Synod 1928*, pp. 61-62; *Acts of Synod 1980*, pp. 42-43, 325-61.)

7.   Prayer is a kind of "loving communion" with God. Share with others in your group a time in your life when you felt very close to the Lord, in "loving communion" with him through prayer.

8.   You pray long and earnestly for your child who has leukemia, but the child dies. Or you pray fervently that a loved one may come to know Christ, but she never does. Or you beg God to save your marriage, but it ends in divorce. How do you handle "unanswered" prayers such as these? How can having a "kingdom perspective" help? Share a time in your life when you learned through unanswered prayer that God's grace is sufficient.

9.   One of the best-known Latin mottos is *ora et labora*, "pray and work." On the basis of such passages as 1 John 3:22-23 and James 5:16-18, what would you say is the relationship between prayer and work?

10.  The Commentary rejects the idea of prayer as a blank check that we write out for God to endorse. Yet don't Jesus' words "Ask and it will be given to you; seek and you will find" (Matt. 7:7) point in that direction? On the other hand, when we add the qualifier *whatever we ask according to God's will will be granted* (see 1 John 5:14), don't we limit the assurance that resounds in the words of Jesus? (See also James 4:2-3.)

## EARTHKEEPING

By sovereign appointment we are
earthkeepers and caretakers:
loving our neighbor,
tending the creation,
and meeting our needs.
God uses our skills
in the unfolding and well-being of his world.

(Contemporary Testimony, 10)

When humans no longer show God's image,
all creation suffers.
We abuse the creation or idolize it.
We are estranged from our Creator,
from our neighbor, and from all that God has made.

(Contemporary Testimony, 16)

Pollution of water and air, misuse of land, and abuse of animals and birds are increasing as the human population level of the world rises. In the rush to exploit resources the environment is changed, good farmland is paved, and human well-being is threatened by "nuclear and chemical wastes." Animals suffer the effects of oil spills and of unethical research.

It is not helpful to blame only industry for this mess, for all humans inherited the task of earthkeeping from Adam and Eve. When they were given dominion over the earth and its creatures and allowed to use the creation for food, they were also told to till and keep the garden (Gen. 1:28-29; 2:15). Humans have a unique place in creation because they are its stewards. This task has too often been ignored or misunderstood when economic or selfish motives have won out over the need to conserve the earth's resources for others and to protect its beauty.

Concern for the environment, however, must not lead to an idolatry of nature in its undeveloped state. Creation contains resources and possibilities that can and may be explored for the benefit of all its inhabitants. Stewards must balance the concern about pollution with the needs to mine and use the resources of the earth.

In every way we use the earth, we must remember that it belongs to the Lord. Our priority should be to use it for his glory, obeying his commands. He gave us dominion over his earth, and he expects us to use it with respect and wonder.

11. The Commentary states, "Humans have a unique place in creation because they are its stewards." Stewards act in the name of the Lord, to whom the world belongs. They care for the earth and use it to further their service to God in all areas of life. What difficulties do we encounter in being good stewards of the earth?

12. What evidences of "idolizing nature" do you see in our society?

13. What, practically speaking, can you do on a local level to be a good steward of the earth?

## MONEY: ITS PURSUIT AND USE

By sovereign appointment we are
earthkeepers and caretakers:
loving our neighbor,
tending the creation,
and meeting our needs.
God uses our skills
in the unfolding and well-being of his world.

(Contemporary Testimony, 10)

In our work, even in dull routine,
we hear the call to serve our Lord.
We must work for more than wages,
and manage for more than profit,
so that mutual respect
and the just use of goods and skills
may shape the work place,
and so that, while we earn or profit,
useful products and services may result.

(Contemporary Testimony, 51)

The Christian community is economically diverse. It encompasses the destitute as well as the very rich. The biblical message about the proper Christian attitude toward money, then, must of necessity be a complex one, with applications to very different economic experiences.

But there is also a sense in which there is one simple message: all things come from the hand of the Lord. To the poor this message comes as a word of hope: "Blessed is he whose help is the God of Jacob. . . . He upholds the cause of the oppressed and gives food to the hungry" (Ps. 146:5, 7). To the rich it brings a warning: "Do not store up for yourselves treasures on earth. . . . You cannot serve both God and Money" (Matt. 6:19, 24).

All Christians, rich, poor, and of moderate means, must continually examine their attitudes toward money and economic practices. Where is the line between just and necessary individual, familial, and communal needs and an insatiable, covetous desire for material and social advantage? In what ways does the biblical call to moderation restrain us in this important area of human concern?

All who follow Jesus Christ must submit their economic practices and relationships to the discipline of the gospel. The cries of the poor reach the ears of the Lord of hosts, who plants in the hearts of his people—rich and poor alike—a yearning for an order of living in which hunger and thirst, envy and greed, have no place. No one who longs for Christ's kingdom can be content with patterns of economic injustice. We must not nurture covetous desires, but rather we must cultivate a sanctified discontent with oppression, trusting in God's promise that he wants all of us to be equipped with that which is necessary for lives of obedience to his will.

The gospel brings a special challenge to those Christians who have positions of advantage and responsibility in the marketplace. On every level of economic life—as consumers at the candy counter, owners of small businesses, factory laborers, managers of physical and human resources, decision makers in corporations and agencies—we must curb our sinful desires to get more than our proper portion, to cut corners, to take advantage of the weak and the ignorant, to establish monopolies, to cripple the competition, to use unjust measures, and to perpetuate fraud and deceit. All are called upon to do what they can to provide work for the unemployed and the underemployed and to create wholesome opportunities for cooperative labor, attending especially to the needs of those groups and persons who have often been victimized by economic discrimination.

The pattern of discipleship must affect our individual economic attitudes, as well as our relationship to general processes and structures. We must be guided by God's Spirit as we apply biblical norms to decisions regarding how and where we are to work, as well as to the means by which we earn our wages. Principles of Christian stewardship also apply to the issues of how we spend the money that we earn or otherwise receive. The first biblical claim is that money, goods, and food are to be allocated for the poor; we must "seek first [God's] kingdom and his righteousness" (Matt. 6:33). "Our" money is really God's money, which is held in trust and must be used responsibly.

Christians who are not themselves numbered among the poor ought to make their spending decisions prayerfully in view of the staggering needs of the economically deprived and of those service organizations which rely on Christian moral and financial support. The Christian community should evaluate and support worthy enterprises that Christians have begun in order to meet needs in our society in obedience to the claims of the gospel. Christians can endorse and welcome the attempts of government to meet critical human needs, but Christians cannot leave this task to government. We must support the work of the church and of other Christian agencies in ministering to the needy. This is an essential element of Christian stewardship, which is all the more urgent for us when we see the levels of comfort and luxury which many of us enjoy.

Jesus' conversation with the rich ruler reminds us "how hard" financial obedience to the Lord is; it shows us, too, how crucial such obedience is (Luke 18:18-27). In this practical area of whether and how we make and spend our money, we are encouraged by what our God makes "possible."

(Previous synodical statements: *Acts of Synod 1970*, pp. 40-41, 500.)

14. "Meeting our needs" while "loving our neighbor" captures the dual economic responsibility of Christians. We need to provide for ourselves and our families, while giving generously to those less blessed. In so doing, says the Commentary, we are "encouraged by what our God makes 'possible.'" Are you encouraged by what God has made possible in this area? Talk with others in your group about some of your feelings and experiences.

15. Most Christians readily agree that the story of the rich ruler (Mark 10; Luke 18) does not mean that Christians should sell all their possessions and give the proceeds to the poor. But then what is Christ teaching us by this encounter—merely that we should always be willing to give up everything for him? What does the story say to affluent Christians of today?

16. "All who follow Jesus Christ must submit their economic practices and relationships to the discipline of the gospel," says the Commentary, adding that we may not be content with economic injustice or nurture covetous desires.

    Some Christians are offended by the obvious wealth of other Christians who may live in big houses, drive fancy cars, regularly visit swanky restaurants, take numerous long vacations, and so on. Such displays of wealth are an affront to the poor, the critics charge.

    What do you think?

17. Some Christians believe tithing (giving 10 percent of your income to kingdom causes) is required by Scripture. They point to passages such as Malachi 3:6-12 and Luke 11:42. Other Christians argue that tithing is legal-

istic and that the Christian liberty given by the New Testament requires only generous giving, not tithing (1 Cor. 16:2; 2 Cor. 9:7). What do you think? Is tithing recommended by your church? Should it be?

18. In the materialistic times in which we live, how do you go about teaching your children the proper use of money and the place of possessions? Share some of your frustrations/successes with others in your group.

## SCIENTISM, TECHNOLOGY, GENETIC MANIPULATION

By sovereign appointment we are
earthkeepers and caretakers:
loving our neighbor,
tending the creation,
and meeting our needs.
God uses our skills
in the unfolding and well-being of his world.

(Contemporary Testimony, 10)

Grateful for the advances
in science and technology,
we make careful use of their products,
on guard against idolatry
and harmful research,
and careful to use them in ways that answer
to God's demands
to love our neighbor
and to care for the earth and its creatures.

(Contemporary Testimony, 52)

God made the world, including our human bodies, good and to glorify the Creator. Sin changed the world and radically altered human desire to use that world in the service of God. However, salvation through the death of Jesus Christ has redemptive power both for humans and creation. Creation's redemption is seen when redeemed human beings use it once again in the service of God and study to discover its riches in order to correct the defects in creation which have resulted from sin.

Responsibility for the universe and the efforts to study and know ever deeper secrets of its workings have become an obsession of secular society. Forgetting the God who is the Creator of the world and the Origin of all its complex interactions, this society has come to see science and the technological applications of scientific discovery as systems with their own laws.

We agree that the discovery of new knowledge and the application of this knowledge to correct the disharmony in nature resulting from sin are a part of our cultural mandate and are renewed by the redemptive work of Christ. We deplore the frequency with which new knowledge and the technologies which result from this knowledge are used to increase the bondage of creation and to bring ever greater chaos, suffering, and death to our society. The knowledge which allows humans to release the power of the atom and alter the behavior of cells and organisms by the introduction of new genetic instructions (genetic manipulation) has the potential for great good or incomprehensible evil and suffering.

We remind the Christian community of its responsibility to insist that the fruits of scientific activity be used for good rather than evil. We reject both the antitechnological stance as well as that in which technology becomes an idol. Resources for the pursuit of science must be allocated in such a way that the discovery of new knowledge and technology proceeds at a pace that allows society to develop controls to use these discoveries to the end that God intended them.

We reject, as contrary to God's will, those applications of genetic manipulation wherein genetic material is introduced into the cells of humans to produce new life through asexual reproduction by techniques such as cloning. We acknowledge with gratitude the discovery of techniques for genetic manipulation which make possible the introduction of genetic instruction to cells of the human body which will have the potential for curing many diseases resulting from genetic abnormalities. We urge the Christian community to be diligent in the work of directing the use of such new knowledge toward the relief of suffering and the happiness and health of the human race.

19. In contrast with past times when the church viewed new knowledge with great suspicion, the present church both accepts the importance of scientific discovery and benefits from the technological applications of this knowledge. Certainly God intended that his creatures should learn the secrets of nature. Yet Christians remain divided: some are confident that scientific discovery can solve the problems of our fractured world, while others are concerned that developing technologies can destroy our world. What should our attitude be? How can Christians avoid the idolatry of "scientism"? When should Christians decide a new technology should be either banned or destroyed?

20. This topic generates a number of controversial issues and questions. Pick one or more of the following to debate, using specific cases if possible:
    • When, if ever, may Christians "pull the plug" on life-supporting medical means used to keep a terminally ill patient alive?
    • What should our reaction be to the techniques producing "test-tube babies"?
    • If technology reveals a fetus to be severely malformed, may the pregnancy be aborted? Is so, when?
    • Suppose that ten people desperately need a kidney from a certain donor. How do you determine who gets it?

## Sharing Creation's Gifts

> By sovereign appointment we are
> earthkeepers and caretakers:
> loving our neighbor,
> tending the creation,
> and meeting our needs.
> God uses our skills
> in the unfolding and well-being of his world.
>
> (Contemporary Testimony, 10)

> Following the apostles, the church is sent . . .
> to feed the hungry . . .
>
> (Contemporary Testimony, 44)

An obvious injustice in this age is the continuing contrast between poor and rich. North American and European consumer societies live in luxury; segments within them and whole continents barely scrape by or starve. God has appointed humans as stewards of the creation; each person therefore has to be concerned with justice in access to the products of creation.

The Old Testament instructs God's people in stewardly methods of giving the poor a share in the harvest. Harvesters were told not to reap the corners of their fields, and gleaners were not to glean twice. The food they left was for the poor and the transient (Lev. 19:9-10). When Israel ignored God's ways and "trample[d] on the poor," God warned them of his anger at such selfish injustice (Amos 5:7, 10-11). And in Jesus God stated clearly for all time that his children are to love their neighbors by feeding them (I John 3:10-18; Gal. 6:10).

The same message comes to modern stewards in the complexity of economic and market patterns. The use of resources in one country is related to food supply in another. When wealthy nations use more of the world's goods, they obviously leave less for everyone else.

Therefore we urge all citizens to live with moderation, to fight waste and conspicuous consumption in their own lives, and to remind government of its task in promoting a fair distribution of the earth's resources. As members of the church whose Lord fed the hungry, we are to teach what the Bible says about justice and to reach out to the needy with diaconal help, and we must constantly remind each other that our daily decisions about how we live, what we eat, and how far we drive can affect world economic patterns so that more fellow humans may have a just share of food, shelter, and clothing.

(Previous synodical statements: "And He Had Compassion on Them," *Acts of Synod 1978*, pp. 80-84, 563-632; "For My Neighbor's Good," *Acts of Synod 1979*, pp. 82-84, 610-41.)

21. "That I do whatever I can for my neighbor's good, that I treat him as I would like others to treat me, and that I work faithfully so that I may share with those in need."

    Where would you find the above statement?

    World hunger isn't exactly a new concern. Why does it get so much attention now?

22. What, specifically, might it mean for us to "live with moderation, to fight waste and conspicuous consumption" in our own lives?

23. Are we as a church and as individual Christians doing enough to help feed the hungry of our world? What measures seem to you to be least effective? most effective?


## FEMINISM

Male and female,
all of us are to represent God
as we do our tasks.

(Contemporary Testimony, 11)


Since God made us male and female in his image,
one sex may not look down on the other,
nor should we flaunt or exploit our sexuality.
Our roles as men and women must conform
to God's gifts and commands
as we shape our cultural patterns.

(Contemporary Testimony, 47)

Women reaching adulthood today make choices that faced few women of previous generations. A widening range of educational and job opportunities is open to them, and roles are less firmly fixed. Decisions about careers, marriage, and having and raising children need to be made. Women and men no longer follow automatically the patterns and goals of their parents.

These changes have come through the courageous actions of individuals and groups of women who have worked and suffered so that other women can vote and use their insights and abilities. It must be recognized at the same time that some new opportunities were granted out of necessity, such as female factory labor during the world wars and in an expanding economy.

We regret that this economic aspect still lingers in the misconception, also found in feminist circles, that a woman's work is valuable only when she is paid for it. Our modern society should not claim to have liberated a working mother when the high cost of living forces her to work outside the home. The Christian community should repent of the male chauvinism that easily slips into its humor and attitudes. This is out of place in a fellowship which confesses that God's image is seen in both women and men, especially since this fellowship has been so blessed in the exercise of the abilities of women in education and mission.

We call on men and women to reflect carefully on the Bible's teaching and to pray for the Spirit's guidance so that we may be kept from extreme language, false motives, and sinful reaction. The Christian community which knows that the Bible does not prescribe rigid roles for either sex could well take the lead in fostering appreciation for the task of parenting by father and mother. And while teaching that male and female are made in God's image and that both are given dominion over the creation, the church of Christ is confronted with the challenge to express the unity that male and female have in Christ in its structures and ministries (Gen. 1:27-28; Gal. 3:28). Our efforts should not be for supremacy of one sex over the other, nor for equality in an individualistic sense, but for each person to use her or his gifts most effectively in God's service.

Therefore, while we warn against misuse of the new options open to women, we do rejoice that women now have more vocational opportunity to serve God and their neighbor with all that God has given them.

> (Previous synodical statements: Female suffrage in civic life, *Acts of Synod 1914*, p. 16; Female suffrage in congregational meetings study, *Acts of Synod 1947*, p. 47; Women's right to vote in congregational meetings, *Acts of Synod 1957*, pp. 90, 308ff.; RES report referred to churches, *Acts of Synod 1973*, pp. 82ff., 514-94; Women deacons, *Acts of Synod 1978*, pp. 101-05, 484-533; Women deacons ratification deferred, *Acts of Synod 1979*, pp. 118-22; Headship in the Bible, *Acts of Synod 1984*, pp. 282-376, 654-55.)

24. What do you take to be the meaning of the three lines from stanza 11 of the Testimony, quoted above? What are some of the implications of this statement?

25. The Commentary notes a grave misconception in modern society—that a woman's work is valuable only when she is paid for it. Have you encountered this? Why is such a view so harmful?

26. The Commentary says that "the Christian community should repent of the male chauvinism that easily slips into its humor and attitudes." Can you give some examples of this chauvinism? Do you agree that repentance is necessary?

27. "Women," says the Commentary, "now have more vocational opportunity to serve God and their neighbor" than women did in the past. Do you agree or disagree?

## MARRIAGE AND THE FAMILY

> Male and female,
> all of us are to represent God
> as we do our tasks.
> Whether single or married,
> we are called to live within God's order
> in lives of loving service.

(Contemporary Testimony, 11)

> In marriage and family,
> we serve God
> by reflecting his covenant love
> in life-long loyalty,
> and by teaching his ways,
> so that children may know Jesus as their Lord
> and learn to use their gifts in a life of joyful service.

(Contemporary Testimony, 49)

The current increase of divorce, trial and common-law marriage, adultery and casual sex, and marriage breakdowns in the Christian community shows that the institution of marriage is not functioning in obedience to God's will.

Marriage was instituted by God at the beginning of history as a covenant between a man and a woman who promise to live together in love and fidelity. God gave marriage to enrich the lives of women and men so that together they can serve better in his kingdom. The image for marriage of the church as the bride of Christ emphasizes the love and permanence which mark this covenant.

Marriage also provides the structure for bearing and raising children. In Christian families children come to know God's will; they see and are taught the ways of his kingdom.

The image of the church as the family of God teaches that the mutual support that is found in the family and in marriage should also be present in our congregations. Whether we are married or unmarried, we are all fully and equally members of a larger family. The church is the place where all of God's children should find love and support and where they are encouraged to use the gifts given to them by the Holy Spirit.

We observe with sorrow that these are hard times for marriages and families. We grieve for the heartaches, the broken homes, and the children of divorce.

In a fallen world that breaks God's design, the church echoes the Lord by recalling the beginning of marriage as a permanent relationship of mutual love and by warning against destructive behavior (Mal. 2:13-16; Matt. 19:3-9). Casual sex destroys the intimacy it seeks and is against the nature of sexual intercourse (1 Cor. 6:15-18). Trial marriage withholds the trust that marriage requires and mocks its covenant character. Divorce is against God's will. Although it is obvious that divorce happens in the Christian community, the church has been reluctant to cite cases and circumstances when it would be allowable. For the emphasis in the Bible is for marriage and against divorce. There are situations where divorce is inevitable, but sorrow and repentance and prior attempts at reconciliation are always necessary. A remarriage after divorce should not conflict with biblical teaching on marriage and divorce nor repeat previous mistakes. Therefore, members who have been divorced should make use of the counseling and teaching ministries of the church to grow in awareness of their own intentions and of the covenant of marriage.

As churches together we should work hard to be congregations where single persons find scope to use their talents and feel at home, where loving families give children the start they need, and where Christian counsel and support surround families and individuals who experience stress.

(Previous synodical statements: "Marriage Guidelines," *Acts of Synod 1980,* pp. 40-41, 467-85.)

28. A recurring theme in the Testimony is that because we live in God's world, not our own, we must see ourselves as God's servants, fulfilling our tasks in his kingdom. This understanding of what it means to be human differs greatly from that held by many people who see themselves as servants only to their own interests. How is this latter understanding reflected in modern marriage and family life?

29. Support the Commentary's statement that the emphasis in the Bible is for marriage and against divorce.

30. Divorce is increasing, even among Christian couples. What, if anything, can the church do to reverse this?

31. How can the church best aid individuals and families who are suffering the results of divorce?

## ABORTION AND EUTHANASIA

No matter what our age, or race, or color,
we are the human family together,
for the Creator made us all.
Since life is his gift,
we foster the well-being of others,
protecting the unborn and helpless from harm.

(Contemporary Testimony, 12)

Sin is present everywhere . . .
in abuse of the weak and helpless . . .
in destruction of living creatures. . . .
We have become victims of our own sin.

(Contemporary Testimony, 17)

We serve Christ by thankfully receiving our life
as a gift from his hand.
We protest and resist
all abuse and harm of this gift
by abortion, pollution, gluttony,
addiction, and all foolish risks.

(Contemporary Testimony, 46)

Although God prohibits killing, this secular society defends the right of the individual or society to determine when life may be ended through abortion or euthanasia.

We recognize that a proper response to these trends calls for the guidance of the Holy Spirit as we conduct a vigorous reexamination of scriptural principles. We affirm the value of all human life, but we acknowledge that there are apparent inconsistencies between this affirmation and permitting at the same time the termination of a pregnancy when it severely threatens the mother's life, or in allowing the withdrawal of artificial or mechanical support systems when brain death has occurred.

We reject, as contrary to God's will, euthanasia and abortion on demand. The history of civilization shows the brutalizing effect of ignoring Scripture's command not to kill. Efforts to produce a master race through eugenics, abortion, and euthanasia have been the prelude to the disintegration of such a society.

The mental, emotional, and physical pain that may be the result of this prohibition against ending life, except in unusual circumstances, must be a constant concern of the church. Since women frequently bear the major burden of an unwanted pregnancy, they deserve an understanding ministry by the Christian community. Those whose bodies are torn with pain from terminal disease also bear a special burden, as do their family and friends. They deserve more than trite expressions of comfort or a few lines from the Bible out of context. We urge the Christian community to include in their programs the development of resources to help with these burdens, such as counseling centers, homes to care for people who are disabled or terminally ill, and scholars to articulate biblical teaching about abortion and euthanasia.

We long for the wisdom that will enable us as confessing Christians to act and speak with corrective hope to our destructive secular society.

(Previous synodical statements: Testimony re abortion, *Acts of Synod 1972*, pp. 63ff., 479-84.)

32. Euthanasia and abortion—planned termination of life—are contrary to God's will. But are they ever permissible? If so, under what conditions? For example, may a Christian, suffering from advanced lung cancer, decide to forgo radiation and other life-prolonging medical treatment? Or, in another case, may the Christian parents of a thirteen-year-old victim of rape decide to end her pregnancy?

33. How can Christians effectively counter abortion? For example, is Christian counseling available in your community for the unmarried and pregnant? Are alternatives to abortion adequately presented? What other measures—such as political pressure, advertising, picketing—should be taken?

34. What kind of Christian help is available in your community for those who have undergone an abortion and are experiencing deep regret and guilt?

## AGING

No matter what our age, or race, or color,
we are the human family together,
for the Creator made us all.
Since life is his gift,
we foster the well-being of others,
protecting the unborn and helpless from harm.

(Contemporary Testimony, 12)

Sin is present everywhere . . .
in abuse of the weak and helpless . . .

(Contemporary Testimony, 17)

We urge governments to ensure the well-being of all citizens . . .
by guarding the elderly and poor . . .

(Contemporary Testimony, 54)

A result of the medical advances in this century is that, at least in Europe and North America, people are living longer. This fact, combined with a lower birth rate, has caused the elderly to comprise a greater proportion of the population.

That shift places new pressures on institutions and retirement benefit plans that serve the elderly.

As people who know the command to "honor your father and your mother" we must confess that we and our society have been so busy with our immediate family, so convinced that only those who produce economic benefits are valuable, and so enamored by the cult of youth that the aged have been retired, out of sight and out of mind, as if they have nothing to offer or to do. We have not adjusted our institutions and ministries enough to include them. We have not thanked God for his gift of long life.

So that we may together keep God's command, we call on families, churches, and governments to protect the elderly from being pushed aside. We welcome laws that allow voluntary retirement and prohibit discrimination because of age. And we urge public institutions and churches to make their programs as open as possible to those who are disabled by their age.

We encourage the elderly to receive their days with gratitude as a gift from God. We urge them not to keep working desperately, as if their only worth to the community or themselves is economic. We ask them not to waste their wisdom in nostalgia for "the old days" (Eccles. 7:10), but to keep their place within the community as much as possible, teaching us wisdom and patience, and reminding us of God's faithfulness.

35. To what extent have the elderly in your congregation or Christian community been neglected, as paragraph two of the Commentary confesses?

36. Find out what percentage of your congregation is over sixty-five. How many of the elders are over sixty-five? What other opportunities for meaningful service does your congregation provide for the elderly?

37. Some of the elderly cannot read small print, hear soft speakers, and walk up stairs. What has been done to help them in your congregation?

38. The elderly, says the Commentary, can teach us wisdom and patience. Describe something specific you've learned from someone over sixty-five. Or, if you are elderly, describe something you've taught someone younger, such as your children or grandchildren.

## RACISM

No matter what our age, or race, or color,
we are the human family together,
for the Creator made us all.
Since life is his gift,
we foster the well-being of others. . . .

(Contemporary Testimony, 12)

Sin is present everywhere—
in pride of race,
in arrogance of nations,
in the abuse of the weak and helpless . . .
in slavery. . . .
We have become victims of our own sin.

(Contemporary Testimony, 17)

The rich variety of human cultures in our world includes the racial and ethnic diversity of humanity. This variety of cultures prevents life from being drearily uniform and allows people with various gifts and resources to respond to their circumstances in their own way.

But different races and ethnic groups have also exploited and enslaved each other. History has seen intensive programs of genocide and discrimination. When racial and ethnic differences become barriers that block understanding and opportunity, the sin of racism is present. Racism is pride in one's own race—and hatred, oppression, or disdain for those who are different. It is opposed to God's demand that we love our neighbor without "favoritism" (James 2:1, 8-9).

God did use the framework of ethnic diversity to work his redemption. He chose a specific ethnic group, the people of Israel, as recipients of his covenant mercies. But this was only one phase of a comprehensive plan of salvation. For God had promised from the first that he would extend the blessings of his covenant to a people which would be formed out of the nations of the earth.

This promise was kept at Pentecost, where the curse of Babel was lifted and people of various tribes and races could hear the one gospel of salvation. Through the blood of Jesus a new community was formed, drawn from the nations, but in which "there is neither Jew nor Greek, slave nor free, male nor female, for you are all one in Christ Jesus" (Gal. 3:28). We long for the day when the nations shall live in unity in the city of God (Rev. 21).

We celebrate our new identity as the people of the Lamb. Since his blood unifies his followers into one body, we can no longer identify ourselves simply in terms of any racial or ethnic blood. Those who by grace have been accepted by God must be accepted by all of God's people. In the body of Christ all schemes for restricting people for ethnic or racial reasons are a denial of the unity for which Jesus prayed and died.

Because of what we have learned at the cross of Christ, we must reject and condemn all forms of racial and ethnic discrimination. We call upon authorities in all walks of life to put an end to methods of oppression or policies of apartheid which continue such discrimination. We repent of our own involvement in these injustices. And we call upon Christians everywhere to work toward the elimination of discriminatory barriers among races and peoples. With the Spirit's help we are to promote healing, especially within the church of Christ.

(Previous synodical statements: Declaration, *Acts of Synod 1959*, pp. 82ff.; Declaration, *Acts of Synod 1968*, pp. 17ff.; "All Nations Heritage Sunday," *Acts of Synod 1983*, pp. 216, 652-53; Apartheid as a heresy, *Acts of Synod 1984*, pp. 601-4.)

39. The Commentary says that "because of what we've learned at the cross of Christ, we must reject and condemn all forms of racial and ethnic discrimination."

a. What have you personally learned (about avoiding discrimination) at the cross of Christ?
b. Do Christians today continue to maintain racist attitudes and practices? If yes, where and how? Give specific examples, if possible.
c. What in your experience has been most effective in combating racism among church members?

## Modern Culture

All spheres of life—
marriage and family,
work and worship,
school and state,
our play and art—
bear the wounds of our rebellion.

(Contemporary Testimony, 17)

Rest and leisure are gifts of God
to relax us and to set us free
to discover and to explore.
Believing that he provides for us,
we can rest more trustingly
and entertain ourselves more simply.

(Contemporary Testimony, 51)

Current expressions of modern culture force each Christian to make judgments and choices. Cultural activities often reveal that, due to secularization, the vestiges of Christian influence on Western culture are disappearing. History also records human violations of divine norms, which were roundly condemned by Israel's prophets. However, this secular society increasingly considers violations to the norm to be normal and acceptable; decency is rare, while blasphemy, violence, and lust are common. The area of culture, therefore, is also a battlefield between the forces of good and evil where the Christian must discern and do the will of God.

In evaluating the visual arts, music, dance, sports, and recreation, it must be recognized that gifts and talents in this area come from God, but that their use is involved in the battle of good and evil. The difference between believers and unbelievers cannot always be detected in their cultural expressions, but it ought to become plain in their motivation and purpose (Rom. 12:1-2). A Christian may accept and enjoy whatever is true, honorable, just, pure, and lovely, but must shun all evil (Phil. 4:8) and avoid giving offense to others. Since unchangeable norms are being applied to changing cultural expressions, the Christian response will vary with time and place. Christians in the pagan Roman Empire and Christians in this secular society follow the same light but travel through different forests. Therefore the spirits must be tested in communal and individual listening to the voice of God and in careful understanding of the trends in modern culture.

One phenomenon that manifests many of the dangerous trends in contemporary culture is organized athletics. Many family members devote significant blocks of time to viewing professional sports events on television. Educational institutions in the Christian community maintain programs in interscholastic athletic competition. The intense interest in sports events sometimes threatens the Christian community and the larger human society in many ways. Idolatrous attitudes and commitments are fostered. Unhealthy rivalries are encouraged. Individuals and families sometimes organize their whole lives around the viewing of, or participation in, athletic activities, and the cycles of work and rest and worship are regularly disrupted.

With the lure of glamour and high income, sports are increasingly commercialized. Human beings are bought, sold, and traded in a manner reminiscent of slavery. Play and recreation are transformed into "big business," and the proper concern for physical fitness is distorted.

Parallel difficulties can also be observed in other activities relating to entertainment and the arts. The film industry seems increasingly interested in catering to tastes and interests which are destructive to Christian values. Much of popular music exhibits violence, nihilism, and rebellion. The visual arts often seem devoted to nothing more than the expression of meaninglessness and disorder.

The Christian community must be sensitive to these trends and to the challenges these trends raise for those who are pursuing lives of discipleship. But it is not enough for us to reject—or to claim to reject—the forms and expressions of "modern culture." We must acknowledge our communal calling to be shapers of cultural patterns and products that will glorify the Creator. The world of human culture also belongs to God.

Therefore we call upon the Christian community to seek new paths of cultural obedience:

- by making stewardly use of present-day opportunities for recreation through the encouragement of appropriate attitudes toward the viewing of and participation in athletic events so that the interest in sports activity and physical fitness may promote enriched lives of Christian service and cooperation.
- by encouraging the critical study of film, music, painting, sculpture, and other art forms, so that the sensitivities of the entire Christian community may be enhanced.
- by giving support to musicians, artists, and filmmakers so that such persons may find opportunity to develop patterns of Christian obedience in these crucial areas of cultural formation.

The Christian response to modern culture may be neither simple withdrawal nor blind acceptance, since God is to be served in all of life. But the hedonism of a society which tries to escape the grim realities of life and ruins its rest with frantic recreation or "entertainment" is to be rejected. Christians must select and form and use cultural expressions that do not involve the breaking of God's law but which praise God for the rest, joy, and beauty he gives to his creatures.

(Previous synodical statements: "Film Arts," *Acts of Synod 1966*, pp. 32ff., 316-61; "Dance," *Acts of Synod 1982*, pp. 89-91, 556-75.)

40. Most of us have more leisure time than we had a decade or two ago, but we also have more things to occupy our leisure time than we used to. Do you generally feel good or guilty about our increased rest/leisure? How does section 51 of the Contemporary Testimony fit with your answer?

41. Review the standards, or criteria, for evaluating modern culture, as mentioned in the second paragraph of the Commentary. Applying these standards, what TV programs would you allow/not allow children (say, from ages 10-15) to watch? Mention some movies you would or would not attend if you took these standards seriously.

42. How much emphasis does your local high school place on athletics/sports? If change is needed, how can it be brought about? Should all Christians be encouraged to follow a program of physical fitness?

43. In what concrete ways can the Christian community encourage writers, artists, musicians, filmmakers, and so on to use their talents for God's glory?

## THOSE WITH DISABILITIES

Sin is present everywhere . . .
in abuse of the weak and helpless . . .

(Contemporary Testimony, 17)

In education we seek to acknowledge the Lord
by promoting schools and teaching
in which the light of his Word shines in all learning,
where students, of whatever ability,
are treated as persons who bear God's image
and have a place in his plan.

(Contemporary Testimony, 50)

The place of mentally and physically disabled persons has changed throughout history as society's perception of disabled persons has changed. Plato and Aristotle thought that the weak and infirm should be discarded at an early age. In the early settlement years on this continent, persons with mental impairments were seen as public problems who needed restraint in jails. Later, in reaction to uncaring treatment of persons with disabilities, many people began to treat them as objects of pity who should be kept out of the mainstream of life. Today, through the work of concerned individuals and agencies, much has been done to correct the injustices suffered by the disabled in our society. Although we cannot claim that the church has led the way in giving mentally and physically disabled persons the care and place they need in society, it is true that those who follow Christ are motivated to minister to the weak and disabled in a just and merciful way.

For in the kingdom of Christ the worth of humans is not measured by their health, wealth, looks, or knowledge. Those in need have always been under God's special care (Ps. 35:10). Jesus shows that he is God's ruler by caring for the needy and by instructing his church to care for them (Ps. 72:12-14; Matt. 11:28-30; Luke

4:18; 6:20-23; James 1:27). In fact, "God chose what is weak in the world to shame the strong" and to puncture our notions of worth and dignity (I Cor. 1:27-28).

Therefore, we are to ensure that persons who have disabilities can take a place in our congregations and communities, which fits the biblical command to show no partiality in our treatment of persons (James 2:1, 9). Persons who have disabilities do not need our pity or condescension, but they may expect that our services and activities are open to their involvement. We may note with gratitude, therefore, that those who are mentally impaired, who were formerly excluded from much of our school and church education, now benefit from such new programs of instruction as the *Friendship Series*. Many of our churches have made great progress in including persons with mental disabilities in their activities and in improving access to and facilities within their buildings for the disabled, including those who suffer hearing or sight loss.

However, we also urge all Christians to minister to persons with disabilities in the community at large. Christ gives us the task to protect the weak and to care for the infirm, wherever they live. We call upon our church members to be active in supporting political and community efforts to foster the well-being of those who are weak and have little influence.

Rather than consider persons who have disabilities to be a burden to society, we are to encourage them to use their gifts within our churches and communities. For Jesus Christ loves them, and he reminds us by his love for the disabled that his gospel of hope and new life is for the weak and for the humble.

(Previous synodical statements: Report 38, *Acts of Synod 1979*, pp. 662-78; Report 33, *Acts of Synod 1981*, pp. 532-46; "Resolution on Disabilities," *Acts of Synod 1985*, pp. 348-52, 702-3.)


44. The second paragraph of the Commentary lists a number of texts to show that the "poor and needy have always been under God's special care." Take time to read these texts aloud and to reflect briefly on their meaning. Did any one text speak to you personally?

45. The Testimony says,
    In education we seek to acknowledge the Lord . . .
    where students, of whatever ability,
    are treated as persons who bear God's image
    and have a place in his plan.
    To what extent does this describe what happens in your local Christian school? Does it describe the education program of your church?

46. The Commentary considers a wide range of disabilities, physical and mental. How does your congregation minister to persons who have disabilities? Is there a class for persons with mental impairments? Is there a ramp to the building to accommodate wheelchairs? Can the restrooms accommodate wheelchairs? How are the hearing-impaired helped? What is done for those with failing sight? If you sense a need in any of these areas, perhaps you can draw up a proposal for your church council.

47. In what ways does your congregation encourage persons who have mental and physical disabilities to use their gifts?

## SELF-SALVATION

> In all our strivings
> to excuse
> or save ourselves
> we stand condemned
> before the God of Truth.
>
> (Contemporary Testimony, 18)

> In our world, bent under the weight of sin,
> Christ gathers a new community.
> Satan and his evil forces
> seek whom they may confuse and swallow;
> but Jesus builds his church,
> his Spirit guides,
> and grace abounds.
>
> (Contemporary Testimony, 37)

The assumption that humans can take care of themselves and find true life on their own is a rejection of or lack of trust in God. Even the most ordinary things of daily living—breathing, walking, sleeping, talking, thinking—are done by virtue of the gift of creatureliness and by God's sustaining power. Life is a gift and a given. And when life has run stuck, when people are weighed down with guilt and suffering, their dependence on God for renewal and restoration is all the more radical.

It is often thought that well-being, wholeness, joy is first of all a goal to be reached by human striving. The *pursuit* of happiness becomes an obsession. The meaning of life is equated with what is achieved in one's career. When a career reaches a dead end because of illness, life is experienced as utterly empty. An elderly person retired from work can feel totally useless.

The difficulty of gratefully receiving God's gift of life becomes painfully manifested in the many attempts to find salvation and security by human effort. Some people attempt to attain ultimate happiness by living a decent, moral life. Others think that true life is to be found in self-realization; this can reduce others to a means to the end of one's own fulfillment. By contrast, others seek life in rigorous self-denial, either in a cult, where even one's identity is sacrificed in ascetic other-worldliness, or in work, where all is sacrificed for the sake of company or career.

All efforts of self-salvation become stranded on the stubborn reality of human feelings. Even if it were possible to avoid failure today, what would eradicate yesterday's failings and their consequences? To persist in the illusion of self-salvation is to remain on the surface of life, looking at the image in the mirror, while carefully avoiding the X-ray of the heart. Thus life becomes marked by superficiality, if not hypocrisy. Either way, a decent and bright exterior can mask a hollow or dark core.

The cross of Christ is the most penetrating X-ray of human existence. There the love of God for sinners becomes manifest through his judgment of sin. There the barricade of true life, that we try to ignore or remove, is uncovered and removed by God in his Son. Living by the grace of forgiveness, of being accepted by the One who ultimately matters, sets us free to live. We no longer need to be self-made. We recognize ourselves as being made and rescued by God. We make the overwhelming discovery that happiness is most basically a precious gift that catches us by surprise and calls us to respond to the Giver in trust, love, and obedience.

48. The Commentary mentions several forms of self-salvation which seem common in the secular world. What forms, if any, can self-salvation take within the redeemed community, the church?

49. Share with others a scriptural or confessional statement that sums up God's gift of grace.

## ISRAEL, ZIONISM

> The Creator pledged to be God
> to Abraham and his children,
> blessing all nations through them
> as they lived obediently before him.
> He chose Israel as his special people
> to show the glory of his name,
> the power of his love,
> and the wisdom of his ways.
> He gave them his laws through Moses,
> he led them by rulers and teachers,
> so that they would be a people
> whose God was king.
>
> (Contemporary Testimony, 22)

To accept the Old Testament as an essential part of Scripture is to give the covenant an integral place in the Christian life. This brings with it a deep concern for the people of the old covenant, the Jewish people. In the history of redemption, they are a highly privileged people: "Theirs is the adoption as sons; theirs the divine glory, the covenants, the receiving of the law, the temple worship and the promises. Theirs are the patriarchs," and from them the Christ was born (Rom. 9:4-5).

The question of the present role of the Jewish people in God's plan of redemption is difficult to answer. The advent of Zionism, the founding of the state of Israel, and centuries of persecution culminating in the extermination of six million Jews combine to make the question all the more pressing and baffling.

It is simplistic to ascribe the Holocaust to "Christianity," when, in fact, that tragedy sprang from a pagan ideology of blood, soil, and race. It is equally simplistic to exonerate Christianity of all guilt. That this horror could occur on a continent where the vast majority professed faith in Christ remains a permanent blot on the record of Christianity. Furthermore, what can erase the previous history of the persecution of Jews in the name of Christ, supposedly sanctioned by his blood ("Let his blood be on us and on our children!" Matt. 27:25)? What of the conversions of Jews coerced by the sword? It is lamentable but not surprising that for many Jews today the cross is the symbol of persecution.

Zionism, an international movement founded in 1897, is in part a reaction to anti-Semitism. Its goal is political: the organization of a Jewish homeland in Palestine. With the creation of the state of Israel in 1948 this goal was attained. The pressing question for Christians is whether and how this event is part of God's plan of redemption. To answer that question, we must first consider whether the Jewish people continue to have a unique role in God's redemptive plan.

Some say that the New Testament church, regarded as the New Israel, replaced Israel. This is misleading. The people of the old covenant are not simply discarded, or supplanted by the "church." The New Testament knows of no such discontinuity. Gentiles are incorporated into the body of "charter members," the Old Testament people of God. Paul speaks of grafting wild shoots (Gentiles) into the natural olive tree (the Jewish people). He calls attention to the strangeness of this operation—it is contrary to nature.

Correspondingly, Gentile Christians must live and work in the expectation that Jewish people will be grafted back into "their own olive tree" (Rom. 11:17-24). Paul expected the full inclusion of the Jewish people into the new people of God (Rom. 11:26). Accordingly, his first stop on the mission field was the synagogue. We are not bound by this pattern. The long history of alienation between Christians and Jews creates a new situation. Yet the church must demonstrate in its life and mission that in Christ God has indeed broken down "the dividing wall of hostility" (Eph. 2:14).

We must acknowledge that persecution and coerced conversion have formed what appears to be a granite mountain between the Jew and the Messiah. Many Jews are stumbling over rocks we have strewn on their path, so that they stumble long before reaching the only decisive "stumbling stone" (Rom. 9:32). In such situations, we leave to God the judgment as to the blame for the nonconversion of Jewish people. Our responsibility is clear. Before we call them "enemies of God as regards the gospel" (as Paul dares to do), we must ask: Have they clearly seen and heard the good news through us? To the extent that we are not clear and living letters (2 Cor. 3:1-5), we are enemies of the gospel. Meanwhile, there can be little doubt as to how we are to regard the Jewish people, namely, "as far as election is concerned, they are loved on account of the patriarchs" (Rom. 11:28).

What does this mean for the "religious" status of the Jewish people today? They have a unique place in that they are the people of the Old Covenant. That covenant has not been abrogated nor its promises annulled. Consequently, God still claims the Jewish people through the Scriptures originally given to them. Their own sacred writings, therefore, call them to recognize Jesus, their fellow Jew, as the promised Messiah. This is true of no other people. Consequently, when Jews accept the promise fulfilled and surrender to God's claim, they are delivered from the futile attempt to be just before him by works of the law. Thus they may experience the joy of salvation by grace and recognize that all people of "faith are blessed with Abraham," that by faith in Jesus the Messiah they, together with non-Jews, are "Abraham's seed, and heirs according to the promise" (Gal. 3:9,14, 29). Furthermore, following a fellow Jew as the Messiah, they need not abandon everything in their heritage but may recover for themselves and for Gentile Christians the true riches of the Old Testament covenant, fulfilled in Christ according to the New Testament.

Must we attach special significance to the existence of Israel as state? After the persecutions that culminated in the Holocaust, the founding of the state of Israel provides a haven for the Jewish people. There is no biblical warrant, however, for regarding the settlement of a minority of the Jewish people in the state of Israel as a special facet of God's plan of redemption. It is striking that even in his most direct and passionate response to the question of the destiny of the Jewish people (Rom. 9-11) Paul not once mentions the land. This does not mean that land is insignificant. For the Jews as a people it is highly significant in view of the injustices they endured in "dispersion." Furthermore, in the Scriptures the promise of land is never replaced with a promise of heaven. It is simply enlarged to encompass a renewed earth (Rev. 11:15).

Under no circumstances may the special status of the Jews as people of the covenant be used as sanction for injustices within Israel or for acts of aggression beyond its borders. Like any other nation, Israel is subject to norms of justice. Violation of those norms cannot bring security or blessing.

(Previous synodical statements: *Acts of Synod 1958*, pp. 23-24, 138-52; "Principles and Guidelines for Jewish Evangelism," *Acts of Synod 1971*, p. 59.)


50. Is modern Israel in any sense a "special people" of God?

51. Do you agree with the Commentary's observation that "there is no biblical warrant . . . for regarding the settlement of a minority of the Jewish people in the state of Israel as a special facet of God's plan"? Why or why not?

52. How do you react to the Commentary's assertion that "many Jews are stumbling over rocks we have strewn on their path"?


## ELECTION AND REPROBATION

Being both God and man,
Jesus is the only Mediator
between God and his people.
He alone paid the debt of our sin;
there is no other Savior!
In him the Father chose those
whom he would save.
His electing love sustains our hope:
God's grace is free
to save sinners who offer nothing
but their need for mercy.

(Contemporary Testimony, 28)


The doctrines of election and reprobation have been the subject of much discussion within the Christian Reformed Church. These teachings also mark a crucial difference between Reformed and some other evangelical churches. We gladly testify now why we keep teaching these doctrines.

The Bible shows that God works out his own design as he reclaims the world for himself. The redemption of sinners is accomplished by the amazing grace of the sovereign God, who initiates salvation. Our faith, love, piety, or good works do not force God to favor us. In fact, we confess that from the beginning of our life on earth we need the forgiveness and renewal of God's mercy. But we celebrate the freedom of God to save those who do not deserve it.

So the church confesses that the elect patriarchs, Israel, and the church were chosen in Christ "to grace and to glory, to salvation and to the way of salvation . . . " (Canons of Dort, I, 8). We know and believe this because God has shown it in the proclamation of the gospel. To believe in Christ is, through the working of the Holy Spirit, to believe in God, who has elected us in Christ to be his own and to remain his own forever. In God's electing love we see the eternal source of our hope, comfort, and joy (Eph. 1:3-14).

Those sinners who do not come to repentance and faith stay under God's judgment (John 3:18, 36). God is righteous in this judgment, for he is not the cause of sin and unbelief. Rather, he calls sinners to faith and repentance and states his desire that sinners turn and live (Ezek. 33:11). Therefore no sinner who fears that he is reprobate needs to lose hope of salvation, for anyone may turn to Christ and be saved (John 3:16; Canons of Dort, II, 5; III-IV, 8).

In teaching the doctrines of election and reprobation we reject the attempt to find a logical balance between the two. We do not accept Arminianism, which compromises the sovereignty of God, nor fatalism, which denies the responsibility of humans. We trust in the good pleasure of our heavenly Father and gladly teach how long and strong our tie to God is. "For from him and through him and to him are all things. To him be the glory forever!" (Rom. 11:36).

(Previous synodical statements: H. Boer Gravamen, *Acts of Synod 1980,* pp. 73-76, 486-558.)

53. The doctrine of election/reprobation has been one of the most misunderstood teachings of the Reformed church. How do you respond to these Arminian misunderstandings, restated from the conclusion of the Canons of Dort?
    a. Election encourages sinful living, since people feel secure in their salvation, regardless of how they live.
    b. Election . . . can lead to despair for those who strive to be obedient but fail.
    c. Election makes God into an "unjust tyrant who by a mere arbitrary act of his will has predestinated the greatest part of the world to eternal damnation. . . ."
    d. Election makes God the author of sin; just as election causes faith and good works, so reprobation causes unbelief.
    e. Election allows for the damnation of infants of Christian parents, should such children die.
    Perhaps you can add other misunderstandings of election which you've heard or which you've felt.

54. The Testimony and the Commentary both stress the comfort and hope that the teaching of election gives. How do you react to the last four lines of section 28 of the Contemporary Testimony? What is the most reassuring biblical text on election that you know?

## SYNCRETISM

> Being both God and man,
> Jesus is the only Mediator
> between God and his people.
> He alone paid the debt of our sin;
> there is no other Savior!
>
> (Contemporary Testimony, 28)

Syncretism is the attempt to combine different beliefs or religions into a new unit. A secular age that has no room for revealed truth displays syncretistic tendencies from the university classroom, with its comparative religions approach, to the Hare Krishna disciple, who claims to serve Jesus too.

The most obvious syncretism takes place in cults with Christian roots, such as Jehovah's Witnesses, Mormons, or Moonies. They accept some of the Bible and some Christian doctrines but add their own source of truth and new teachings. Church members who belong to secret societies also attempt to live within two communities, each with its own way of salvation. Cults influenced by Eastern religions, such as Baha'i or Hare Krishna, accept Jesus as one of the prophets, but offer a totally different description of and solution to humanity's spiritual problem. Some Christians try to marry the Bible's demand for justice to a revolutionary Marxist analysis of history and social problems, others attempt a marriage of biblical stewardship to unrestrained capitalism, and others turn Christianity into a civil religion.

Two themes recur in many expressions of syncretism. First, a works righteousness is preferred to salvation by grace. Human pride seems to find God's grace demeaning and suggests ways in which persons can save themselves. Second, the difference between the Creator and creatures is blurred. People are taught that they partake of the divine and that by various techniques they can reach enlightenment and unity with the divine.

We must resist and reject syncretism because it denies the clear statements of the gospel. Sadly enough, humanity is so lost in sin that only a miracle of grace can save us. God has incarnated that miracle in Jesus, and the Scriptures say definitely that "salvation is found in no one else, for there is no other name under heaven given to men by which we must be saved" (Acts 4:12). The apostles defended that truth at the risk of their lives; the church today can do no less if it wants to preserve this good news for a broken world.

Pantheistic worldviews which blur the difference between God and humanity deny the biblical account of the creation of humans as God's covenant partners. While searching for salvation by downplaying humanness, these beliefs lose the real dignity that God gives to the crown of creation (Ps. 8). There is no hope in a system that ignores the reality of creation and history and denies that people are human.

We urge all Christians who deal with people of other religions and lifestyles to examine the approaches and teachings of these adherents for syncretistic elements. We certainly respect sincere efforts to hear and understand other religions, and we share the love for fellow human beings shown in these efforts. We may indeed see a response to God's revelation in all religions (Rom. 1:19-20; 2:15). But we warn against all relativizing of the uniqueness of Jesus Christ and of God's revelation in the Scriptures. If in our love for followers of other religions we ignore the fact that they also "suppress the truth by their wickedness," and do not present them with the claims of Jesus, our tolerance would turn out to be most unloving, for we would fail to introduce them to the one who said of himself: "I am the way and the truth and the life. No one comes to the Father except through me" (Rom. 1:18; John 14:6).

> (Previous synodical statements: Basic position on the lodge, *Acts of Synod 1974*, pp. 58ff., 547; Confessional commitment of lodge members, *Acts of Synod 1977*, pp. 102-6, 575-96.)

55. What are some of the fundamental doctrines at stake in syncretistic situations?

56. What attracts young people, including some brought up as Christians, to such cults as Jehovah's Witnesses, Mormons, Moonies, Baha'i, or Hare Krishna? What is the best antidote to the temptation to move in syncretistic directions?

## THE LAITY

> The Spirit thrusts
> God's people into worldwide mission.
> He impels young and old,
> men and women,
> to go next door and far away
> into science and art,
> media and marketplace
> with the good news of God's grace.
> The Spirit goes before them and with them,
> convincing the world of sin
> and pleading the cause of Christ.
>
> (Contemporary Testimony, 32)

One of the most radical tenets of the Reformation is the priesthood of all believers. It arose directly out of the rediscovery of the Bible, justification by faith through grace, and the rejection of all mediating agencies or persons. If one cannot be set right before God through good works, nor through a sacramental system dispensed by a priestly class, but only through faith in the gospel, then in Jesus Christ the believing community itself stands directly before the face of God. The priesthood of all believers means a total rejection of the distinction between a priestly class with special access to God and his grace (the clergy) and a lower class of people (the laity) which is dependent on the mediation of this higher class.

The universal priesthood is attested directly in 1 Peter 2:9, and even more powerfully in Romans 12:1. Here it becomes clear that by the grace of God each Christian is at once a priest ("*offer* your bodies") and a sacrificial offering ("offer *your bodies* as living *sacrifices*"). Moreover, this priestly sacrificial service is not restricted to a realm of "religion" or the church. By grace, believers are called to be priests in all of life: "offer your bodies" (that is, one's entire flesh-and-blood existence) as a thank offering to God. The whole of life is to be presented "holy and acceptable" before God.

To bring out the various aspects of the full service made possible in Christ, the office of all believers has also been elaborated as a threefold office: royal, priestly, and prophetic. As priests we stand in God's presence and dedicate ourselves to him, serve our neighbor, and intercede for the world. As royalty we are called and equipped to rule our affairs in Christ's name. As prophets we uncover and declare God's will for daily life.

The rediscovery of the office of all believers by the Reformers led to the rejection of any division of God's people into first-class and second-class citizens of the kingdom. In all of life the tutelage by the clergy and the instituted church was broken. The effect of this breakthrough can be seen where Christians, independently of clergy and church, seek to uncover the meaning of reconciliation in Christ in areas such as education, journalism, labor, politics, and business.

In spite of this radical break with clericalism, the reformation of life has in many ways stalled at this point. For too often Christians look to the minister not so much to equip *them* to read and understand Scripture, but to read the Word *for* them. The minister becomes the high priest of interpretation. Soon "the laity" are unable to discern whether the minister is rightly reading the Word "for" them. As a result a stirring homily, or a flashy presentation that is only tenuously related to Scripture, can be mistaken for the Word of God.

It is ironic that within the church the office of all believers has not come into its own. As a historian has pointed out, the office of all believers was permanently secured only in congregational singing. (In the pre-Reformation church the sacred songs were chanted in a sacred tongue, Latin, by a sacred class, the priests.)

A first step toward the recovery of the office of all believers is the resolute rejection of the clergy/laity distinction. But that, of course, is not enough. Practices and notions that seem to confirm this distinction must be abolished.

First of all the notion of office itself needs clarification. It is telling that no exact equivalent of our term *office* is found in the New Testament. Instead it speaks of *diakonia*, service or ministry. This service is committed to the entire church, not to a select group of individuals. This does not exclude specialized "ministries" or "services" rendered by individuals appointed for that purpose.

> From the beginning these particular ministries were functional in character, arising under the guidance of the Spirit in the interests of good order and efficiency in the church, to enable the church to carry out Christ's work in the world most effectively. *(Acts of Synod 1973*, p. 63)

To break the legacy of clericalism we also need to understand the relationship of office to ordination and authority. Since the Bible does not connect "ministry" primarily with "status, dominance, or privilege" but with service, ordination does not elevate a person to a social and higher class (*ordo*).

> "Ordination" should be understood as the appointment or setting apart of certain members of the church for particular ministries that are strategic for the accomplishment of the church's total minority. *(Ibid.)*

Both the primacy of the office of all believers and the serving character of special office do not abolish but qualify the authority that inheres in office. The only head of the church is Jesus Christ (Belgic Confession, Art. 31). He rules his church by his Word and Spirit. Hence the authority of one in special office with respect to the community of believers is not that of one person having dominance over another. The authority of special office is the authorization to give leadership in submission to the Word of God in the task to which he or she is appointed. Required for that kind of leadership is not an authority that dominates but the authority that presupposes discernment into the leading by the Lord through his Word. There is no room for any other lordship. There is room for no other Master (Matt. 23:8-12; Luke 22:24-27).

(Previous synodical statements: "Guidelines for understanding the nature of ecclesiastical office and ordination," *Acts of Synod 1973,* pp. 61-64, 635-716; *Acts of Synod 1976,* pp. 46, 602ff.; *Acts of Synod 1979,* pp. 47-49, 510-18; *Acts of Synod 1980,* pp. 43-45, 559-71.)

57. What practices, if any, tend to confirm a clergy/laity distinction in the Christian Reformed Church? What practices have you observed that break down the clergy/laity barrier and build up the office of all believers?

58. How does the Bible help us avoid too rigid an authoritarian pattern on the one hand and too loose a democratic approach on the other? (See, for example, Matt. 23:8-12; Luke 22:24-27; Heb. 13:17; Rom. 13:1-7.)

59. When people speak for or against women in office, how do different ideas of "office," "authority," "ordination," and "service" affect their positions on this issue? How do passages such as those mentioned in question 58 help to clear up some confusion on both sides of the issue?

60. "Soon 'the laity' are unable to discern whether the minister is rightly reading the Word 'for' them. As a result a stirring homily, or a flashy presentation which is only tenuously related to Scripture, can be mistaken for the Word of God" (Commentary).
    To what extent do you think the above is true in the Christian Reformed Church? Is the laity no longer able to judge the scriptural soundness of a sermon? If not, what has contributed to this inadequacy?

## NEO-PENTECOSTALISM

The Spirit's gifts are here to stay
in rich variety—
fitting responses to timely needs.
We thankfully see each other
as gifted members of the fellowship
which delights in the creative Spirit's work.
He gives more than enough
to each believer
for God's praise and our neighbor's welfare.

(Contemporary Testimony, 33)

Pentecost is celebrated as the day on which the Holy Spirit was given to the church, just as promised to Israel and to Christ's disciples. Although the church has always celebrated this feast, the pentecostal tradition which arose in North America at the beginning of this century gave new attention to baptism with the Holy Spirit and to the gifts of tongues and healing. When neo-pentecostalism arose more recently, it created a new situation within Protestant and Catholic churches by importing these pentecostal emphases.

It must be admitted that the church has often reacted to this phenomenon with poor grace, and, conversely, that many who criticized the church for alleged stifling of the Spirit did so with little charity. This did not provide a climate for mutual encouragement and understanding.

Neo-pentecostalism is also known as the charismatic movement, because it emphasizes the "charismata," the gifts of the Spirit. Two factors occur in most charismatics: first, they look back on their life in the church before their charismatic experience as bleak, empty, and poor—conditions which the regular ministry of the church was not able to heal. Second, they have found spiritual renewal and vigor in the emphasis on baptism and filling by the Spirit, on prophecy, healing, and tongues-speaking.

The church should note frankly that the charismatic renewal has alerted all of us to the resources that the Spirit makes available to each believer. Our Christ-centered theology, prayers, hymns, and practices have been invigorated by these reminders of the Spirit's indispensable role in the new life.

We regret, at the same time, that much confusion and hurt have been caused. Pentecost indeed ushers in the new age of the Holy Spirit, whose gifts are given to each believer. The New Testament lists a variety of gifts (Rom. 12:6-8; 1 Cor. 12:8-10; Eph. 4:11). There is no fixed list of gifts. The Spirit distributes them according to the need of the hour. It is confusing, then, to select a few gifts as proving the presence of the Spirit in a believer's life. An elitism is also fostered when one set of gifts (the so-called second blessing: healing, prophecy, tongues) is used to create classes of believers. Fellow believers, who by faith are in Christ and therefore also "in the Spirit," are hurt, and the unity of the work of Christ and the Spirit is denied (2 Cor. 3:17).

We rejoice that all believers are gifted (1 Pet. 4:10-11). We commit ourselves to greater tolerance and encouragement of each member's gifts in lively worship, encouraging fellowship, caring outreach, and down-to-earth obedience. With thankful hearts we claim the assurance that our daily lives may be "in step with the Spirit" (Gal. 5:25). The power of the Spirit refreshes our energy, bends our stubborn wills, and helps each of us to love God and our neighbor in our own unique way. God is still with us and active in his world! For that we praise Father, Son, and Holy Spirit.

(Previous synodical statements: Neo-pentecostalism, *Acts of Synod 1973*, pp. 71-79, 398-493; Neo-pentecostalism and office-bearers, *Acts of Synod 1974*, pp. 31, 623-25.)

61. In what sense did the outpouring of the Holy Spirit usher in a new age? Was it a once-for-all, unrepeatable event? Were the gifts of prophecy, tongues, and healing limited to the apostolic age, or are they still with us today? How is the Spirit still active among us today?

62. Is neo-pentecostal criticism of the church justifiable? Has the movement generally had a positive or negative influence on the church?

## INERRANCY

> The Bible is the Word of God,
> record and tool of his redeeming work.
> It is the Word of Truth,
> fully reliable in leading us
> to know God
> and have life
> in Jesus Christ.
>
> (Contemporary Testimony, 35)

> The Bible tells God's mighty acts
> in the unfolding of covenant history.
> It is one revelation in two Testaments,
> which shows a single plan of salvation,
> and reveals God's will infallibly.
> As God's people hear the Word and do it,
> they are equipped for discipleship,
> to witness to the good news:
> Our world belongs to God
> and he loves it deeply.
>
> (Contemporary Testimony, 36)

In answer to modern criticism of the Bible the evangelical Christian community has vigorously defended the historic doctrines of the inspiration, authority, and infallibility of the Bible. As evangelicals engage in this defense, they themselves have been divided over the insistence that inerrancy offers a firmer test of faith than infallibility.

The basic thrust of the term *inerrancy* has been acceptable to the Christian Reformed Church; this is seen in the statement that Scripture is "infallible in its total extent and in all its parts" (*Acts of Synod 1961*, p. 124). When both terms are understood as a confession of the full trustworthiness and reliability of Scripture, that it is without error in its disclosure of the history of redemption, *inerrancy* and *infallibility* are nearly equivalent terms.

But some consider *inerrancy* to be the stronger affirmation. They then look for a precision and accuracy in biblical revelation that meets the standards of modern historiography. Weaknesses in this view are that preconceived notions of inerrancy may be imposed on the Bible and that the central purpose of the Bible may be slighted.

However, we acknowledge gratefully that adherents of infallibility and inerrancy take the Bible seriously as the foundation for Christian faith and life. For the crisis of secularism demands a firm biblical commitment by modern Christians. For us, as for the Reformers, Scripture is *necessary* for knowing the truth, it is *sufficient* for salvation, it is *clear* in its witness to Jesus Christ, and it is *authoritative* for living the Christian life. Therefore the church has confessed that "we receive all these books, and these only, as holy and canonical, for the regulation, foundation, and confirmation of our faith; believing without any doubt all things contained in them . . ." (Belgic Confession, Art. 5).

We affirm, therefore, the value of biblical scholarship, and we discourage efforts to make it suspect by playing off the plain reading of Scripture against hermeneutics. We must state honestly that all reading of Scripture is accompanied by interpretation; scholar and secretary should help each other to interpret obediently.

A great threat to Bible-centered living is that the secular spirit of our times causes neglect of the Bible in the life of the Christian community by narrowing the area in which we use and apply it. We must not let endless debates about inspiration and infallibility stand in the way of actually hearing and doing God's Word in our daily life. Talking about Scripture is not a substitute for obeying it.

Modern believers may be sure that God will still use the Bible to show the way. For we have God's assurance that "the word of our God stands forever" (Isa. 40:8). In that unfailing Word we trust.

(Previous synodical statements: Infallibility and Inspiration, *Acts of Synod 1961*, pp. 76-79, 253-328; Nature and Extent of Biblical Authority, *Acts of Synod 1972*, pp. 66-69, 493-546).

63. Both the Testimony and its Commentary stop short of complete acceptance of the evangelical view of inerrancy as implying a precise and accurate and error-free revelation that meets the standards of modern historiography. What are your reactions to this? Is *inerrancy* a stronger test of orthodoxy than *infallibility*, or are the terms nearly equivalent?

64. React to the following statement in the light of your own opinion and the remarks made in the Commentary:

I believe the Bible speaks plainly to ordinary people like myself. It means exactly what it says. We shouldn't always go running to commentaries or to "experts" who tell us what some word meant in Greek or who talk about the "original audience" or "historical setting" of a passage. We ought to just read the Bible with the Spirit guiding us. Then we can get on with the most important thing—*doing* what the Bible says instead of just endlessly talking about it!

## DISPENSATIONALISM

The Bible tells God's mighty acts
in the unfolding of covenant history.
It is one revelation in two Testaments,
which shows a single plan of salvation,
and reveals God's will infallibly.

(Contemporary Testimony, 36)

Dispensationalism originated in the Brethren movement, which John Nelson Darby, the Father of dispensationalism, joined in the 1820s. Dispensationalism was disseminated by the Scofield Reference Bible, an edition of the King James

Bible with notes by C. I. Scofield. In these notes the history of redemption is divided into seven dispensations. A dispensation is "a period of time during which man is tested in respect of his obedience to some specific revelation of the will of God." The touchstone of dispensationalism is a sharp distinction between Israel and the church in the literal reading of prophecy. It teaches that Jesus offered the Jewish people a restored theocracy on earth. When the Jews rejected this Davidic Savior-King, the messianic kingdom was postponed, and the dispensation of the church was interposed. Although the church includes Jewish people as individuals, God's plan for the Jews is to be fulfilled during the millennium, when Christ will reign over a primarily Jewish kingdom (all believers having been translated to heaven in the rapture that preceded). Temple worship will be restored, although the sacrifices are memorial rather than propitiatory offerings. At the end of the thousand-year reign of Christ within the theocracy, the heavenly Jerusalem (the abode of the resurrected saints) will come down to earth, the judgment will take place, and the new heaven and earth will be ushered in.

While many regard the future as lying either in the hands of human beings or at the mercy of chance or fate, dispensationalism reminds us that Christian hope is directed to the visible, bodily return of Christ. Moreover, in the insistence that the promise concerning a coming kingdom concerns a concrete kingdom on earth, we recognize the good news that God has not abandoned this earth. Christians too often understand the kingdom as spiritual and "unworldly," i.e., strictly personal and internal. Finally, in pointing to the varied ways of God's dealing with his people in varied circumstances (Adam, patriarchs, theocracy, Jesus, New Testament church), dispensationalists show an awareness of the historical nature of redemption.

These positive elements, however, lose their effect in dispensationalism as a system. The future-directedness feeds one's curiosity rather than setting one to work to welcome Christ. The emphasis on the literalness of the kingdom is robbed of its relevance because that kingdom is strictly future. The structure of God's kingdom on earth is identified with one historical phase of God's dealing with his people, the Old Testament theocracy. Moreover, by contrasting the concrete with the spiritual, dispensationalism fails to recognize both the spirituality of the Old Testament kingdom and the concreteness of the kingdom that has come and is present in Christ.

Dispensationalism disfigures the history of redemption. Some dispensationalists teach that after the patriarchs, God deals with his people primarily on the basis of law and works. This ignores God's gracious dealing with Israel and his constant call for faith and trust. This distortion carries over to the millennium. For not only is the Davidic theocracy to be reinstituted, but the temple and its sacrificial rites as well.

Finally, the relevance of the coming kingdom is focused on a plot of ground in the Middle East. The suffering of Christians today is slighted in favor of speculation about a final tribulation—which Christians will escape. The spiritual but earthly meaning of the struggle between the forces of darkness and of light in the present and future is obliterated by stunning scenarios of the great future conflagration—Armageddon.

In summary, dispensationalism errs in the following ways:

1. By promoting a literalistic reading, dispensationalism fails to see the full literal intent of prophecy and thereby fragments the Scriptures.

2. By losing sight of the unity of the Scriptures, dispensationalism breaks up the unity of redemptive history into contrasting "dispensations."

3. Besides restricting the earthliness of the kingdom to the theocracy of the Old Testament and the future millennial kingdom, dispensationalism shunts cultural and societal responsibility of Christians to a dead-end track.

By contrast, the Reformed confessions reflect the unity of Scripture by insisting that the one holy catholic church of Christ "has been from the beginning of the world, and will be to the end thereof" (Belgic Confession, Art. 27; cf. Heidelberg Catechism, Q&A 54). In accordance with this confession, the Christian Reformed Church advocates a redemptive-historical approach to the Scriptures. This understanding of God's Word attempts to do justice both to the variety and the unity of God's ongoing work of redemption. Moreover, the Reformed understanding of the kingdom as the implementation of God's intention and will for creaturely life maintains the tension between the (literal) inauguration of the kingdom in Christ and its (literal) consummation upon Christ's bodily, visible return. Within that tension, we are called to live out of God's reconciliation of the *world* and work as its agents.

(Previous synodical statements: Report 44, *Acts of Synod 1972*, pp. 66-69, 493-546.)

65. What is meant by the "redemptive-historical" approach to the Scriptures, an approach which the CRC advocates and dispensationalists reject? What are the implications of this view for life today and for the consummation to come?

66. What biblical passages would you use to refute the view that the nation of Israel will be singled out in some special way during the millennium? Or, to put the question positively, what biblical evidence is there that the church of Christ is the "Israel" of the New Testament and that God's promises to Israel now apply to all believers?

67. Much debate among conservative Christians has centered on the proper interpretation of the millennium, or thousand-year reign, of Revelation 20:4. Perhaps you've heard of *a-mil, pre-mil,* and *post-mil* views. What do these terms refer to? Has the CRC officially adopted a position on the questions these terms answer? Does it tend to support any particular view?

# The Occult

Satan and his evil forces
seek whom they may confuse and swallow;
but Jesus builds his church,
his Spirit guides,
and grace abounds.

(Contemporary Testimony, 37)

A strange evidence of the spiritual bankruptcy of our secular age is the current interest in the occult. Movies, books, and plays deal with Satan and evil spirits. Astrology and fortune-telling are still popular. Psychics offer seances in shopping malls, horoscopes are printed in the daily paper next to the comics, and young people are intrigued by occult games and music.

While some of these practices may not seem satanic by themselves, they do feed a fascination with the unknown and can provide openings for evil forces. For the Bible warns that we are in a spiritual struggle between Christ's kingdom and the kingdom of darkness (Eph. 6:12). Christ came into this world to "destroy the devil's work" (1 John 3:8). He defeated the evil one by his death and resurrection; we may participate in the victory when we are "wise about what is good, and innocent about what is evil" (Rom. 16:19-20). God has made us his possession by living in us with the Spirit; we can resist the evil one with the confidence that we are not in his grip (James 4:7-8).

The attraction of the occult may begin with play or curiosity, but it becomes a search for another source of knowledge and power. God has warned his children away from "spiritists, who whisper and mutter," and from divination (Isa. 8:19-20; 2:6). We must be content with the revealed Word of God: it is clear and complete enough to let us know God's will and to guide our living. As creatures before the Creator we must display a becoming modesty and realize that the secret things belong to God. A child of God would show a rebellious and discontented spirit by seeking access to superhuman powers and by courting the help of Satan and the demonic world.

Since Christ has delivered us from the tyranny of darkness, it is foolish and dangerous to play games with the enemy. Therefore we have been taught to pray, "Lead us not into temptation, but deliver us from the evil one" with the assurance that the kingdom, the power, and the glory belong to our Lord forever.

68. What are the reasons behind the current fascination with the occult?

69. What forms of the occult are in evidence in your community? What should be the Christian attitude toward these occult activities?

## LITURGY AND WORSHIP

> Our new life in Christ
> is celebrated and nourished
> in the fellowship of congregations
> where God's name is praised,
> his Word proclaimed,
> his way taught;
> where sins are confessed,
> prayers and gifts offered,
> and sacraments are celebrated.
>
> (Contemporary Testimony, 39)

> The Spirit empowers each member
> to take part in the ministry of all,
> so that hurts are healed
> and all may rejoice
> in the life and growth of the fellowship.
>
> (Contemporary Testimony, 41)

Our century, and especially the last two decades, has seen more liturgical renewal than any time since the Reformation. This renewed interest in liturgy is both legitimate and understandable. Churches of the Reformation had also developed their rigid tradition of worship. The pastors again became the main doers of the liturgy, and the people were often spectators. The Lord's Supper was separated from regular worship, and each church and denomination had settled for a tradition of worship that offered the blend of intellectual, emotional, and aesthetic elements it found fitting.

We rejoice that the Reformed churches kept the basic structure of worship: God speaking to his people in the reading and preaching of his Word, and the people answering in their songs, prayers, and offerings. This essential liturgical dialogue continued to occur, even though traditions stifled some of the human voices.

In our age worship needs the sensitive attention of the church. For to worship and thank God and to invite others to join us in praising God remain the abiding tasks of the church. Therefore, liturgy, which gives shape and order to our common worship, needs the church's study of our traditions and of the needs and gifts of the day. In our cities, where the hour of worship may be one of the few times when believers are together with other believers, the encouraging, fellowship dimensions of worship need to be developed (Heb. 10:23-25). In our largely secular times, in which believers are confronted by faith in machines and techniques, we need the nourishing reminder in the sacrament that Christ alone saves us by his grace; we need the happy reassurance and the encouraging reality of worship that shows that the new life has begun (Rom. 12:1-3; Eph. 5:19). As we become more aware that God is gathering the nations into the church, we need patterns of worship that allow the whole church to recognize the cultural diversity of the body of Christ. As life becomes more regimented, the church needs to be a free fellowship where each believer's gifts can be used to God's praise and where guilt-ridden, frustrated lives can be liberated by his Word.

Many people consider rituals to be the essence of worship and, therefore, would never tamper with them. A more open vision emerges from the Scriptures (1 Cor. 14:26, 40; Col. 2:16-19)—a vision of a fellowship that praises God with "order" and with a desire to "strengthen" its members, while using the gifts that God has given to each. In planning its worship each congregation will want to give due care that the biblical elements of worship are present: God's Word; our prayers, hymns, gifts, and confessions; and the sacraments in which God's actions and the response of his church are combined in true covenantal style.

Every believer and every congregation are called to the exciting task each week of offering the unique adoration and praise that the local situation and gifts make necessary and possible. For "great is the Lord and most worthy of praise" (Ps. 96:4).

(Previous synodical statements: *Acts of Synod 1928*, pp. 60-61; Liturgical Report, *Acts of Synod 1968*, pp. 134-98; The second service, *Acts of Synod 1973*, pp. 505-43; Church Music, *Acts of Synod 1979*, p. 607.)

70. Examine the usual order of worship in your morning service and pick out the "liturgical dialogue." In which parts of the liturgy does God speak? In which do his people respond?

71. Read Hebrews 10:23-25, noting the "fellowship dimensions" of worship that the passage suggests. What's being done in your congregation to enhance this aspect of worship? Does "fellowship" need to be emphasized more—or less—in your congregational worship?

72. What changes in liturgy have you witnessed during your lifetime? Do these changes generally please you, or are you upset by them? Comment.

73. "As we become more aware that God is gathering the nations into the church, we need patterns of worship that allow the whole church to recognize the cultural diversity of the body of Christ" (Commentary).

What patterns of worship in your congregational liturgy demonstrate the cultural diversity of the body of Christ? Why is it important to demonstrate this?

74. What is the most important part of the liturgy? The sermon? The sacraments? The praise rendered to God by the congregation? Comment.

## THE SACRAMENTS

God meets us in the sacraments,
holy acts in which his deeds
elicit our response.
God reminds and assures us in baptism,
whether of those newly born or newly converted,
that his covenant love saves us,
that he washes away our guilt,
gives us the Spirit,

and expects our love in return.
In the supper our Lord offers
the bread and cup to believers
to guarantee our share
in his death and resurrection,
and to unite us to him
and to each other.
We take this food gladly,
announcing as we eat
that Jesus is our life
and that he shall come again
to call us to the Supper of the Lamb.

(Contemporary Testimony, 40)

The traditional understanding and celebration of the sacraments are being called into question in various ways. Infant baptism is challenged, on the one hand, by the insistence that salvation requires a conscious personal decision for Christ and, on the other hand, by the practice of rebaptizing those who claim an experience of being "baptized by the Spirit."

There can be no question of the need for an intense personal commitment to Christ and the new life given by the Spirit. Without faith in Christ and a continual openness to the renewing presence of his Spirit, baptism may be viewed as an automatic gateway to the kingdom of God.

At the same time, those who reject or devalue infant baptism must ask themselves whether they have not unwittingly "shortened" the saving arm of the Lord by making his redeeming activity dependent upon individual decisions. In this way, disregard is shown for his saving work through patterns and structures created and given by him—for example, the gift of family and nurture. God chose to establish his covenant with his people by way of families (Gen. 15:1-6; 17:1-8). In the New Testament God does not deal with his people in a radically different way (Acts 2:39; 1 Cor. 7:14; 2 Tim. 1:5). He does not negate but rather fulfills the old covenant.

Baptism, then, does not in and of itself "create" a Christian. Baptism is a visible affirmation by God of his promises. Baptism as an instrument of God's grace realizes its purpose only when it is trustingly and obediently received by the community of faith. The community surrounds the parents and child with prayer and loving support as the child is nurtured in the context of the pledged promises of the God of salvation. As children grow up, they must be urged to accept the gift of God's sealed love in Christ and to trust God's rich promises. Infant baptism is not at odds with but wholly directed to personal commitment.

Similarly, the refreshing and renewing power of the Holy Spirit that some experience in a dramatic way does not detract from the meaningfulness of infant baptism. Rather, the innovative operation of the Spirit in the lives of believers is evidence that God does deliver on his promises, whether by a sudden conversion or by a slowly blossoming faith. To seek rebaptism by water, therefore, is to bring into question the significance of the sacrament. One thereby may reduce baptism to a symbol of one's personal commitment of faith and of a new experience of the Holy Spirit's power.

The practice of restricting participation in the Lord's Supper to those who have publicly confessed their faith is being challenged on the basis of the covenant. Since children are added to the covenant family by God, it is argued, they should not be excluded from the table that the Lord prepares for that family. In this view, baptized children who believe and trust in Christ as their only Savior must not be deprived of the spiritual nourishment and festive celebration of the Lord's Supper. This approach implies that the responsibility for the supervision of the table of the Lord is shared by the congregation, consistory, and parents.

Both the baptism of infants and the issue of children at the Lord's table point us to the truth that God's redemptive acts are bigger than our individual decisions and reach deeper than our conscious experience. God works in community and surrounds, evokes, and nourishes our faith by means of grace. The sacraments are visible signs and tangible seals of a saving God whose arm is long and powerful.

A number of difficult questions arise today with regard to the church's faithful practice of the sacraments:

What leads people who were baptized as infants to seek rebaptism as adults?

Who decides when a child is ready to partake of the sacrament?

What would then be the function of profession of faith?

At what age would profession of faith occur?

How often should the Lord's Supper be celebrated in our liturgical services?

If the Lord's Supper is a true means of grace, then what accounts for hesitancy in increasing its frequency?

The celebration of the Lord's Supper envisions the spiritual renewal of the community of believers. In view of this, how should we judge the growing practice of sharing the bread and wine outside the congregational setting, for example, in spiritual retreats, consistorial conferences, ministers' institutes, and synods?

The Lord's Supper also strengthens the unity of faith among all followers of Christ. In view of this, how must we view the celebration of this sacrament in ecumenical gatherings of Christians from various churches?

(Previous synodical statements: Adult Water Baptism, *Acts of Synod 1971*, p. 162; Rebaptism, *Acts of Synod 1973*, pp. 74, 77-78; Children at Communion, *Acts of Synod 1984*, pp. 419-24, 651; Intercommunion, *Acts of Synod 1974*, p. 57; Covenant Children at the Lord's Supper, *Acts of Synod 1986*, pp. 617-20; *Agenda for Synod 1986*, pp. 340-70.)

75. The Commentary (above) offers a number of interesting—and difficult— questions for discussing the sacraments.

## THE CHURCH: ECUMENICAL AND INSTITUTIONAL RELATIONS

We grieve that the church
which shares one Spirit, one faith, one hope,
and spans all time, place, race, and language
has become a broken communion in a broken world.
When we struggle for the purity of the church
and for the righteousness God demands,
we pray for saintly courage.

When our pride or blindness blocks
the unity of God's household,
we seek forgiveness.
We marvel that the Lord gathers the broken pieces
to do his work,
and that he blesses us still
with joy, new members,
and surprising evidences of unity.
We commit ourselves to seeking and expressing
the oneness of all who follow Jesus.

(Contemporary Testimony, 43)

A major change for each congregation since the Reformation is the number of other churches that surround it and the variety of ways in which it can relate to other institutions such as the school or the state. This diversity can hamper the mission of the church and runs counter to Jesus' prayer that "those who will believe in me . . . may be one" (John 17:20-21).

Diverse theologies and insights have caused divisions in the church. Some divisions were necessary to return it to biblical foundations; others arose out of human error and stubbornness. At times the institutional church has identified itself too closely with the policies of a national government; at other times it has not found ways to be a prophetic influence in human affairs.

This confusion has caused some to consider the church outmoded or unnecessary. They prefer unstructured movements, cults, or small groups around a dictatorial leader. Others surrender to agnosticism or indifference.

We admit that we have sinned against others who confess the Lord Jesus by misrepresenting their words and deeds and by fostering a climate of competition and animosity. We admit too that all our talk about church as institute and organism can delay our real engagement with the challenge to follow the Lord as his people everywhere.

Nevertheless we believe that the church is instituted by the Lord. All who are called by him belong to the church. The church is the people of God, which shows itself to be an organization which the Lord endows with offices and gifts, and to which he gave instructions for order (Eph. 4:11; 1 Tim. 3). Therefore, no Christian ought to withdraw from the church; all should rather use their gifts to build up the body and to restore its unity.

This century has seen the rise of ecumenical activity. Attempts are made to bring churches together in organizations out of which fellow Christians can speak to the world with a united voice. There have also been several church unions. While church unity is an ideal that is hard to realize, it may not be ignored. But unity must not be based on cultural identity, self-interest, or secular norms for organization; faithfulness to God's Word is the test of true ecumenicity. Its purpose is not prestige or power, but a more faithful obedience to the Lord's commission to go into the world as a teaching, baptizing, and helping church.

So that the church may be free to do its task, it must appeal to governments and international organizations to maintain the freedom to worship, especially on the Lord's day, and the freedom to evangelize.

The church must call individuals to salvation, but it must also call the nations and their leaders to be obedient to God's will for the daily affairs of humanity. The church may not be directly involved in national or international politics as an institution, yet she must inspire her members to be the light of the world, to show compassion, to battle evil and injustice, and to promote the rule of Christ everywhere. Christians who may serve Christ freely without fear of persecution should pray for those who can serve only at great risk.

We pledge ourselves to work for Christian unity and a witness that is disciplined by sound doctrine and nurtured by true piety and that will show itself in words and deeds which honor the only liberator and ruler, Jesus Christ.

(Previous synodical statements: Churches in ecclesiastical fellowship, *Acts of Synod 1974*, pp. 50, 342ff.; Ecumenical Charter proposed, postponed, *Acts of Synod 1985*, pp. 237-41, 728-29).

76. The Testimony asks God's forgiveness "when our pride or blindness blocks the unity of God's household," then goes on to marvel at God's blessing us with "surprising evidences of unity." What signs, if any, of disunity do you see within your own congregation? Is disunity caused by "pride or blindness" or by a genuine "struggle for the purity of the church"? What evidences of unity do you see in your congregation?

77. The Commentary notes a recent increase in the rise of ecumenical activity and then lists some standards for church unity. Using this as a starting point, discuss what your congregation and denomination are doing to seek and express "the oneness of all who follow Jesus. "

78. According to the Commentary, "The church may not be directly involved in national or international politics as an institution," yet it must "call the nations and their leaders to be obedient to God's will for the daily affairs of humanity." How is the church to accomplish this task? What has proven to be most effective? least effective?

## MISSIONS

Following the apostles, the church is sent—
sent with the gospel of the kingdom
to make disciples of all nations,
to feed the hungry,
and to proclaim the assurance that in the name of Christ
there is forgiveness of sin and new life
for all who repent and believe—
to tell the news that our world belongs to God.
In a world estranged from God,
where millions face confusing choices,
this mission is central to our being,
for we announce the one name that saves.
We repent of leaving this work to a few,
we pray for brothers and sisters
who suffer for the faith,
and we rejoice that the Spirit
is waking us to see
our mission in God's world.

(Contemporary Testimony, 44)

The living God reaches out to his fallen, rebellious world, redeeming and reclaiming it. In love God sent his only Son, Jesus Christ, to save the world and to return it to his rule. The Spirit of God is sent into the world to convict it of sin, righteousness, and judgment and to equip disciples to follow the Master. Missions, therefore, spring out of the saving work of the triune God.

The church is used by the Spirit to do missions. In contrast to secular wisdom, which claims the world for humanity, the church must broadcast worldwide that God still rules and that his saving rule alone can bring well-being to the people of the earth. The church is an agent of the Spirit to point the world to God. Where many deny or ignore God, the church must witness to his presence, power, and demands.

Since the Word of God brings life, the gospel must be told to the billions of people who do not know the name of Jesus.

As the firstfruits of God's harvest, the church must show the new life publicly. In word and deed the reality of forgiveness, resurrection, and new direction must be evident.

Each local congregation must be active in evangelism/mission in its own community. And every member must in some sense advance the mission of God in his or her job, family, church, and community activities. The whole church must be involved with the gifts of each member in mission outreach, evangelism programs, and serving ministries.

New believers whom God adds to the church must be accepted warmly into the congregation and should be allowed to use their gifts and insights too. Churches which come into being through missions should not be kept in a dependent position but should be accepted and encouraged to be a fully responsible church of Christ.

As we do our mission, we should avoid a worldly dependence on wealth, numbers, organization, and technique. We may use the new forms of communication but must beware that our life and worship do not become secularized. Even so, it is our conviction that we, in churchly fashion, must continue to use the electronic media to reach the billions of people who now inhabit the world, many of whom can be reached in no other way. The electronic church also can be a blessing for shut-ins and those who will not enter a church, but it cannot replace the powerful effect of the worship and fellowship of a congregation. Professions will also be needed in missions, but to leave this work only to professionals would rob each believer of the dignity of his office.

Modern missions are carried on in a secular world that even tries to relativize religion. The religious options available to each human being are reduced to human likes and dislikes. In this gray world the church must proclaim the clear truth of the only Savior, Jesus Christ, and it must call women and men to repent and believe in him as revealed in the Bible.

Since the Bible reveals God's way of salvation and brings people to Christ, Bible production and distribution are crucial to the mission of God's people. Organizations that translate and distribute the Bible should be supported and encouraged. In the face of the flood of literature produced by cults and other religions, the church of Christ should be diligent and innovative in telling biblical truth in books, tracts, magazines, and other media.

We call God's people to sustain their mission by faithful reading of Scripture, by prayer, by preaching, and by mutual encouragement. We must constantly remind each other of our dependence on the Spirit of God, who can breathe life into our mission activity. In the face of rebellious and secularizing trends in our time we must make it clear that the gospel is the gospel of the kingdom. In Christ's name we may claim all areas of life for him; we must proclaim to every person that Jesus is Lord, inviting them to submit to his life-bringing rule by repentance, faith, and obedience.

As we do the work of mission, we are sustained by the hope and assurance of this vision: "The kingdom of the world has become the kingdom of our Lord and of his Christ, and he will reign for ever and ever" (Rev. 11:15).

(Previous synodical statements: Mission Principles, *Acts of Synod 1977*, pp. 90-94, 614-37; Evangelism Manifesto, *Acts of Synod 1977*, pp. 32, 638-43.)


79. How is the concept of missions rooted in the very nature of the God whom we serve?

80. "Each local congregation must be active in evangelism/mission in its own community," says the Commentary. Review what your congregation is doing to reach the community with the gospel, and evaluate its effectiveness.

81. What does it mean to use electronic media "in churchly fashion" to reach our world with the gospel? Have you ever urged a co-worker to watch *Faith 20*? Why can't the electronic church ever be a substitute for the worship and fellowship of the congregation?

82. Have we, as the Testimony suggests, tended to leave the work of missions to a few? What can the individual church member do to advance the cause of Christ in this world?


## SUBSTANCE ABUSE

We serve Christ by thankfully receiving our life
as a gift from his hand.
We protest and resist all abuse and harm of this gift
by abortion, pollution, gluttony,
addiction, and all foolish risks.

(Contemporary Testimony, 46)

Recent decades have seen an explosion of substance abuse. Even though the risks are well known, narcotic and psychotropic drugs, alcohol, and tobacco are still used in alarming quantities. The media push this abuse in advertising and music and film.

The presence of sin in God's good creation has led to this abuse by altering creation's internal harmony. Plants became weeds, bacteria and viruses produced disease, and animals and people became predators. In his mercy God allowed the discovery of chemicals and other substances to cure disease or to ease pain and to change the behavior of the human mind. But this secular society has misused these discoveries, which can in most cases be used for good or evil. Greed leads to the demand for more powerful weed killers, which can increase the harvest but also cause disease. The wish to escape reality leads to alcohol and drug abuse. And the need for pleasure drives to new thrills with unknown risks.

We grieve at the emptiness of a society that has so much, wastes what it has, and keeps grasping for more. We deplore the physical abuse, the suffering, and the burden to society that is produced by this misuse.

We urge the Christian community to be active in efforts to control substance abuse. We favor continued legal control of dangerous drugs. In view of our community's practice we ask the smokers among us to think hard about the harm they cause themselves and others. We encourage Christians to examine their goals and motives in their living and partying. For although this insatiable modern need for kicks may be hindered by legal means, it can best be opposed by a vital Christian life of joy and meaning at work and at play.

(Previous synodical statements: Testimony on the Liquor Problems, *Acts of Synod 1963*, pp. 87-88; Guidelines on Use of Alcohol and Other Drugs, *Acts of Synod 1986*, pp. 668-71; *Agenda for Synod 1986*, pp. 371-421.)

83. What are some of the causes behind our society's high incidence of substance abuse? How can substance abuse be most effectively prevented? Share what you know about successful programs/approaches used in your community.

84. Agree or disagree: the Christian Reformed Church should officially encourage all of its members to abstain from alcoholic beverages.

85. A lengthy report to Synod 1986 on the use of alcohol concluded that alcoholism is "a biochemical genetic disease. The alcoholic is a carrier of a disease that was genetically handed down to him and that he may hand down to one or more of his offspring. . . . Alcoholism is a primary disease. It is not a symptom of another problem. . . . The alcoholic cannot not drink. . . . While he is morally culpable for the behavior he manifests as a consequence of his drinking, he is not morally culpable for the development of the disease alcoholism." How do you react to these statements? What are the implications of such a stance for the prevention and treatment of alcoholism?

86. What are some ways your local congregation can act as a healing community to individuals and their families suffering from the consequences of alcoholism and other substance abuse?

## DISTORTIONS OF SEXUALITY

Since God made us male and female in his image,
one sex may not look down on the other,
nor should we flaunt or exploit our sexuality.
Our roles as men and women must conform
to God's gifts and commands
as we shape our cultural patterns.
Sexuality is disordered in our fallen world;

grief and loneliness are the result;
but Christ's renewing work gives hope
for order and healing
and surrounds suffering persons
with a compassionate community.

(Contemporary Testimony, 47)

Sexuality was created by God for the enrichment of human relationships. Therefore sexuality is experienced as an integral part of being human. Intimate sexuality in both its physical and psychical senses was created by God as the basis for entering marriage relationships (Gen. 2:20-25).

Sexuality is an area of life in Western societies that is highly susceptible to disorder and abuse. Rape, prostitution, sexual abuse, and incest are not new phenomena, but they appear to be on the increase. Neither is pornography peculiar to our time; yet, technological advances in print, film, and video, combined with a general increase in sexual permissiveness, have made pornography increasingly accessible, profitable, and violent. Abuses of sexuality result from distortions, which in turn lead to dehumanization.

When sexuality is reduced to the individual's physical sensation, rather than the expression of a committed relationship between a man and a woman, it reduces human beings to sexual objects. Distorted views of sexuality teach women to use sex as a way to gain acceptance with or power over men, who in turn measure their own worth according to their sexual prowess. Prostitution takes this concept of sexuality to the extreme by making it a commodity for buying and selling.

Further, if sexuality is seen to be a purely physical sensation, then the search for new sexual sensations will make violence and child involvement seem more desirable. Although there are other factors that contribute to rape, abuse, and incest, distortions of what sexuality means make such acts seem more acceptable.

Similarly, pornography relies more and more on violence toward women and on child abuse. While the depiction of sexuality in writing or in the visual arts is not wrong in itself, pornography delights in a dehumanized view of sexuality that is taken out of its created context.

Christians can support efforts at more stringent enforcement of laws to curb sexual abuse and violence (cf. Contemporary Testimony, 54). We can also encourage more positive images of sexuality in the media. But we must express those positive views especially in our homes, schools, and church communities. In these settings we can revise distorted views of sexuality and celebrate it in the spirit of "The Song of Songs."

(Previous synodical statements: *Acts of Synod 1971*, pp. 541ff.; *Acts of Synod 1972*, pp. 396ff.; *Acts of Synod 1973*, pp. 50-53, 609-33; Dance and the Christian Life, *Acts of Synod 1980*, pp. 459-60.)

87. "Sexuality is disordered in our fallen world," says the Contemporary Testimony. Discuss specifically how some TV programs (or movies) contribute to distorted views of sexuality. Can you mention any programs or movies that promote a healthy view of human sexuality?

88. What are some of the key things Scripture teaches us about sexuality? (A few passages to check include Gen. 2:20-25; Song of Songs 1; 1 Cor. 7:1-9; 1 Thess. 4:3-8; Heb. 13:4.) How can we model biblically faithful patterns of sexuality in the way we talk and act in our homes, schools, and church communities?

89. How should we counsel artists in the Christian community to promote healthy views of sexuality? For instance, is it legitimate for a Christian artist to paint or sculpt a nude? May a Christian writer narrate a lovemaking scene in a novel? When do such portrayals become pornographic or offensive to Christian sensitivities?

## HOMOSEXUALITY

Sexuality is disordered in our fallen world;
grief and loneliness are the result;
but Christ's renewing work gives hope
for order and healing
and surrounds suffering persons
with a compassionate community.

(Contemporary Testimony, 47)

Sexuality is the most intimate area of human relationships; all of us are vulnerable and prey to temptation in this sensitive area. Since our Lord said, as he addressed a situation of sexual infidelity, that only those without sin may cast the first stone, we intend to comment on homosexuality with restraint, humility, and compassion.

The church has learned to see that homosexuality (having an erotic attraction for persons of the same sex) is "a condition of disordered sexuality which reflects the brokenness of our sinful world and for which the homosexual may himself bear only a minimal responsibility" (*Acts of Synod 1972*, p. 51). Homosexualism is explicit homosexual practice; the person engaging in such acts is responsible.

The Scriptures make it clear that intimate sexual expression is proper only within a faithful heterosexual marriage (Ex. 20:14; Rom. 1:26-27). We must therefore warn against all violations of this norm, including those which occur in homosexualism.

Since it appears that a homosexual person's responsibility for his or her condition is minimal, we confess that Christians have acted and spoken out of ignorance toward brothers and sisters who suffer this disorder. They have sometimes been treated in an unloving and cruel manner. This lack of understanding may have driven some into the trap of the "gay" community, where God's directives are not heard and this disorder is considered an alternative lifestyle.

The Christian community should offer its pastoral and counseling ministries to help homosexually inclined persons in their struggle with temptation and sin. The Christian community should be a community where the gifts of such members can be used too, and where they receive friendship and acceptance without suspicion or gossip. Here too it is of vital importance not to be a false witness against our neighbor, and to speak the truth in love. Aware of the demonic promiscuity in our day and of the importance of good family relationships for the healthy development of our children, we call on all Christians to examine their own sexual attitudes and practices in the light of God's Word.

Because homosexual activity distorts the God-ordained patterns of social and family relationships, we urge persons of homosexual orientation to seek the help of the pastoral and counseling ministries of the Christian community in order to arm themselves against temptation and sin. We urge them to take their rightful place in the Christian community and to be patient with its failings and with their condition. We call on those who practice homosexual acts to repent and to seek forgiveness and healing in the hope-filled conviction that it is possible for them to join those who were washed, sanctified, and justified "in the name of the Lord Jesus Christ and by the Spirit of our God" (1 Cor. 6:11).

(Previous synodical statement: Report on homosexuality, *Acts of Synod 1973*, pp. 50-53, 609-33.)

90. Is the distinction between homosexuality (as an orientation) and homosexualism (as a practice) a helpful one? Explain.

91. Has the Christian community sinned against homosexuals by its words, attitudes, and deeds, as the Commentary confesses? What are some positive ways the church can minister to homosexuals more effectively?

92. How should we view the current AIDS epidemic that has hit homosexuals so viciously? Is it right, for example, to think of this terrible disease as a specific judgment of God against homosexuality? Comment.

## EDUCATION

In education we seek to acknowledge the Lord
by promoting schools and teaching
in which the light of his Word shines in all learning,
where students, of whatever ability,
are treated as persons who bear God's image
and have a place in his plan.

(Contemporary Testimony, 50)

Nowhere is the growing secular spirit of our society more evident than in our educational institutions. For at all levels of learning secular humanism has become the dominant philosophy in public education.

Most schools in our Western world were founded on specific Christian ideals. Gradually they drifted into a general theistic position. After the religious and cultural revolution unleashed by the Enlightenment, the Judeo-Christian tradition was forced into a retreat. Now secular humanism has taken over as the dominant shaper of curriculum and pedagogy in most government-supported schools. During this time the church, rightly, became disestablished, but in its place the public school system has become the established religious institution to teach the so-called values of democracy. Under the guise of religious neutrality (which is really a form of practical atheism), secular humanistic education has become the government-preferred education in our public schools.

This secularizing trend in education has placed a heavy burden on many Christian parents. Should the Lord of life be ignored in the education of their children? Therefore many Catholic, Jewish, Lutheran, Reformed, and other Christian communities have founded alternative school systems, often at great cost and under the pressure of unfair taxation. In spite of these obstacles new private schools continue to form, especially in evangelical Christian communities, as citizens react to the spiritual crisis in public education.

In this time of educational ferment we must be firm in our commitment to Christian education as we within the Reformed tradition have come to understand it. In school life we must discern the religious roots of the prevailing secular spirit. For, as the church father Augustine put it, (1) all people serve some god or gods in their lives, (2) people are transformed into the image of their gods, and (3) people then shape societies which reflect their own images and the image of their gods. Our chief concern is, therefore, not the banning of Bible reading and prayers from public education. Nor are we mollified by the toleration of the Bible as literature in some public school studies and by some values-education. The basic problem is the wholesale replacement of a Judeo-Christian worldview by the religious worldview of secular humanism.

As churches we repent of our failure to protest this robbery of our heritage in such a strategic area. We pledge our active intercession for reformation in school and society. We dedicate ourselves to promoting Christian education that follows the biblical principles seen within the Reformed tradition, namely:

- that God, our Father, is the Creator and Sustainer of all,
- that our world with all its creatures belongs to him,
- that he has given us the task of educating as part of the cultural mandate,
- that we are called to exercise the office of believers in teaching and learning,
- that Christian education is called to test the conflicting spirits of our times,
- that, in following Jesus our Lord, we must seek to obey him in thought as well as in deed; in mind, as in body,
- that biblically directed teaching and learning must permeate every discipline and all aspects of school life,
- that Christian education aims at helping all students grow as covenant partners with God, as dwelling places of his Spirit, and as stewards of his creation,
- that we train covenant children to live as kingdom citizens in every calling and in all sectors of society,
- and that in a religiously pluralist society we honor the God-given right of all families to choose the kind of education their children shall receive.

(Previous synodical statements: "Taxation and Christian Education," *Acts of Synod 1975*, pp. 6-8, 609-16.)

93. Schooling in our Western world has drifted from its Christian beginnings; secular humanism is its present dominant philosophy. How could such a radical shift have happened? How have recent court decisions contributed to this shift? Has the Christian community been derelict in its duty in allowing this to happen?

94. What does secular humanism mean in public education? Is the claim of religious neutrality believable?

95. Why have alternative Christian schools been founded?

96. Establishing private, Christian schools is one alternative to exposing our children to the secular humanism of public education. But what about those Christian parents who choose to send their children to a public institution or who teach in the public schools? What contributions can Christian students and teachers make within public schools?

## WORK AND VOCATION

In our work, even in dull routine,
we hear the call to serve our Lord.
We must work for more than wages,
and manage for more than profit,
so that mutual respect
and the just use of goods and skills
may shape the work place,
and so that, while we earn or profit,
useful products and services may result.

(Contemporary Testimony, 51)

Christians see work as more than a means of making a living. They see work foremost as a response to God's calling to care for the creation and each other. They see work as vocation rather than simply occupation. Some are called to minister to human needs for food and shelter, others to produce goods that make life less burdensome and more pleasant. Still others are called to provide such services as education, family nurture, healing, and justice. But in a broken world that suffers the effects of sin and destructive economic forces, some people are forced to accept work that is boring or backbreaking, and some find no work at all.

In view of these workaday problems, the Christian community must promote a view of work that emphasizes the need for every human being to find meaningful activity. In our complex technological society we must increase interest in providing work that serves people and God's creation, without always measuring its profitability. We must encourage a sense of vocation and worth in those who nurture families, and in those who serve society by volunteering their services to charitable organizations.

While temporary unemployment is a normal condition in a mobile society, long-term unemployment reflects a failure of both government and private social and economic structures to move beyond the view of the worker as a profit-making factor. The right to work should be viewed as a fundamental right in a free society. The Christian must call government and society to a higher view of work as the opportunity for every able-bodied man and woman to serve family and/or fellow human beings. Government must promote new work opportunities where the private sector is not providing them.

As Christians stress the dignity and value of work, they must guard against the workaholic syndrome, in which work dominates and distorts life. This is also carried to an extreme in the Marxist glorification of work as the controlling factor in society, which leaves little place for the claims of the family and other societal spheres. Those who work must also be able to rest, to worship, and to follow their interests as citizens and family members.

Christians need to witness to a Christ-centered view of work in the world of labor relations. Labor unions have often been a necessary force in promoting just working conditions in impersonal workplaces. But modern secular unions have too readily sacrificed the quality of work conditions to the narrow goal of more money. Labor and management have failed to search together for meaningfulness in work. Our present structure of labor-management relations does little to foster a sense of common mission and task. It fosters antagonism and conflict instead. Christian employers and employees face an urgent challenge in reconciling broken work relationships. Their individual and communal efforts require the prayers and sympathetic support of God's people.

(Previous synodical statements: Christian Labor Unions, *Acts of Synod 1956*, pp. 105ff.; Corporate Responsibility, *Acts of Synod 1945*, pp. 102ff., 314-26.)

97. What, for the Christian, is the purpose of work? Cite biblical support for your answer, if possible.

98. What are some of the implications of seeing work as vocation rather than simply occupation?

99. Do some careers serve God better than others? Explain.

100. When, if ever, is it permissible for a Christian to change jobs simply because of an opportunity to make more money?

101. In what concrete ways should Christian employers treat their employees differently than non-Christian employers would?

102. What are some of the ways that we can teach our children Christian attitudes toward work?

## Gambling, Lottery

Rest and leisure are gifts of God
to relax us and to set us free
to discover and to explore.
Believing that he provides for us,
we can rest more trustingly
and entertain ourselves more simply.

(Contemporary Testimony, 51)

We call on governments to do public justice
and to protect the freedoms and rights
of individuals, groups, and institutions,
so that each may freely do
the tasks God gives.

(Contemporary Testimony, 54)

As leisure time becomes an increasingly larger part of every person's life in this modern age, the Christian community must become more discerning about the nature of the available leisure activities.

Gambling is one such leisure activity. At one time, commercial gambling was confined to a few vacation spots. Sensitive Christians tended to avoid those spots. However, the increasing popularity of many forms of gambling—from hotel casinos to state lotteries, church bingo parlors, and office sports pools— make a Christian voice on the matter urgent.

Some form of gambling always has been with us despite sporadic efforts to make it illegal. Such efforts have met with little more success than Prohibition Era efforts to make drinking illegal. Even the Christian community has not been unified in its view of gambling. Bingo games and "Casino Nights" remain a favorite fundraising tool in some church circles. Other Christian groups have condemned all forms of gambling as an imposition on God's providence—a view that sweeps so broadly as to condemn many children's games.

Viewed from a Christian perspective, gambling is at best a morally questionable activity. It thrives on the love of money and promotes the unwarranted enrichment of the few at the expense of the many. God has entrusted each of us with resources. As stewards of those resources, whether great or small, we must use them for the well-being of self, family, and fellow human beings. God has given us hands, hearts, and minds to use these resources creatively and productively. The investment of even a small portion of the resources God has entrusted to us in regularly playing the numbers game or in the weekly purchase of lottery tickets violates every notion of Christian stewardship.

Although modest gambling as a form of entertainment or as a charitable fundraising technique may not involve violations of Christian stewardship obligations, the Christian must be extremely wary of leisure activities or fundraising techniques that exploit the human weakness for money (1 Tim. 6:9-10) and seduce the poor with dreams of instant wealth. The horseracing track, the church bingo parlor, the office football pool, the lottery—all generate a measure of excitement through an appeal to a person's baser instincts.

Although the Christian community must not hesitate to speak clearly to the evils of gambling, it must not expect governmental authorities to legislate stewardship. Many other forms of economic activity also violate Christian concepts of stewardship and promote greed and the idolization of wealth. Nevertheless, the Christian community must demand that the state, as the guardian of public justice, carefully regulate commercial gambling where it does exist and refrain from promoting gambling through state lotteries. The state may only promote activities, such as education, physical fitness, and the arts, that clearly advance the well-being of society. Government lotteries violate the state's responsibility to raise revenue in a way that meets minimal standards of distributive justice. A state revenue program may seek to raise money based on the ability to pay, benefits received, or the consumption of certain goods or services. But no state may leave the collection of its revenue to chance.

(Previous church statements: *Acts of Synod 1928*, pp. 86ff.; *Acts of Council of CRC in Canada*, Nov. 1981, pp. 70-71.)

103. What are the motives behind gambling, and how do they violate biblical principles?

104. "Modest gambling as a form of entertainment or as a charitable fundraising technique may not involve violations of Christian stewardship obligations . . . " (Commentary). Give some specific examples of this sort of "modest gambling." When does gambling become something to avoid?

105. Is it wrong for a Christian to occasionally participate in a state or provincial lottery? Why or why not? If such lotteries are wrong, how can Christians more effectively protest them?

## GOVERNMENT AND ECONOMIC JUSTICE

Since God establishes the powers that rule,
we are called to respect them,
unless they trample his Word.
We are to obey God in politics,
pray for our rulers,
and help governments to know his will for public life.

(Contemporary Testimony, 53)

We call on governments to do public justice
and to protect the freedoms and rights
of individuals, groups, and institutions,
so that each may freely do
the tasks God gives.

(Contemporary Testimony, 54)

The whole creation is the kingdom of God—the area where he rules. All creatures are his servants (Ps. 119:91). His law governs our personal lives, but also the government with its economic policies.

God's judgment descended on the human community when it rebelled against God's good order for life in society. This rebellion is evident in broken human relationships, which can take shape institutionally in political injustice and economic suffering.

But this is not the last word. In Christ God set out to restore his righteous rule among persons and groups of people, among communities in society (such as families, schools, and churches), and among associations (such as labor organizations, businesses, and clubs). The quality of renewed living in all these societal structures now depends on our obedient response to the biblical norms for kingdom living.

This kingdom vision must guide us in considering the political norms that hold for governmental policies in promoting economic justice. For God "loves righteousness and justice" (Ps. 33:5). He therefore calls us to image him in dealing justly with all men, especially the needy and disadvantaged. For "with righteousness he will judge the needy, with justice he will give decisions for the poor of the earth" (Isa. 11:4).

In the public life of society the central command of love calls for neighborly justice. For "what does the Lord require of you? To act justly and to love mercy and to walk humbly with your God" (Mic. 6:8). The official task of administering public justice evenhandedly for all citizens is entrusted to government. "By me kings reign," says God, "and rulers make laws that are just" (Prov. 8:15). This is the basis for a just society. It involves a special concern for those who have no voice, the poor and powerless, for widows, orphans, and strangers (Ps. 72:1, 4).

Our starting point in fostering economic justice is the psalmist's testimony, "The earth is the Lord's, and everything in it, the world, and all who live in it" (Ps. 24:1). In light of this, we have no absolute right to private property. God holds charter rights to all the wealth and resources of creation. We are called to be faithful stewards of all we hold. Public goods, too, are always a gift of God's grace.

Governments must enact laws which help to open ways of serving the needs of the weak and helpless, the aged, disabled, and unemployed. It must use its authority and power in the interest of economic stability and equity. It must safeguard the right and responsibility of all persons and institutions to the social space needed to exercise their God-given calling in life. All must be assured of equal access to law and of protection by it.

Government has a limited task. It may not take over the mandate of business and industry to provide needed goods and services. But it may regulate these for the well-being of society—to protect the rights of workers, investors, consumers, and the environment. Government cannot grant these rights, for they are God-given. But it must recognize, honor, preserve, and nurture them impartially.

Government must help prevent the growth of one sector of society at the expense of another. It must avoid alliances with power structures which squeeze the life out of those who lack political and economic influence. Neither national self-interest nor the vested interests of powerful pressure groups may determine its policies. Within the framework of international justice, it must promote a free and open society, where righteousness, peace, and equal opportunity prevail for all citizens and institutions.

Government must not function as a broker of competing parties, but as the referee of good order. Totalitarian claims by the state, notions of popular sovereignty, the tyranny of majoritarian rule, or the romantic ideology of an unrestricted marketplace may not eclipse the sovereign Word of God as the norm for societal life.

In its taxing and spending policies government must seek to counteract the spiraling cost of living brought on by inflation in many parts of the world. Too many people suffer from a runaway economy, especially the poor, the financially insecure, those on fixed incomes, and the elderly. Controlling inflation may not be done at the expense of the poor and unemployed. Its sacrifices must be borne equitably. Government must adopt fiscal policies that tend to avoid great disparities in wealth, thus helping to close the growing gap and to heal the class struggle between haves and have-nots. It should not lend support to the popular ideal of progress, measured in terms of production and consumption, nor allow the GNP to become the chief goal of human life. In levying taxes, government must avoid imposing such heavy burdens upon its citizens that many are stifled in contributing freely to their chosen charities and causes.

Economic justice includes creating conditions which encourage a high level of meaningful employment for all who are able to work. Both nationally and internationally, we must encourage ready access by all people to a fair share in the rich resources of God's creation—eliminating trade barriers that are harmful to poor nations and urging transnational corporations to serve the well-being of native populations.

The Christian community, too, must assume its political responsibilities in promoting economic justice. It must reflect seriously on how to develop a Christian political mind, and then how to rally God's people to create a more effective Christian political presence and witness on behalf of public justice.

(Previous synodical statements: "Taxation and Christian Education," *Acts of Synod 1975,* pp. 64, 609ff.; "Social justice," *Acts of Synod 1978,* pp. 62, 633-43).

106. Review the many tasks the Commentary assigns to government in the area of economic justice. Then discuss what might be some practical ways "to rally God's people to create a more effective Christian political presence and witness on behalf of public justice" (Commentary).

107. Many parents who send their children to Christian schools feel that the government discriminates against them by making them pay for both public and private schools. Is this a problem in your community? What measures, if any, do you think Christian parents can legitimately take to achieve justice in this area? For example, should they refuse to vote for requests from public schools for additional taxes?

108. As you consider your local and national governments, what makes you most grateful?

## SOCIAL STRUCTURES

Knowing that God's people
live under many forms of government,
we are thankful for the freedoms
enjoyed by citizens of many lands;
we grieve with those who live under oppression,
and we work for their liberty
to live without fear.

(Contemporary Testimony, 53)

We call on governments to do public justice
and to protect the freedoms and rights
of individuals, groups, and institutions,
so that each may freely do
the tasks God gives.

(Contemporary Testimony, 54)

The human community is divided by conflicting economic and political loyalties. Many citizens of Western societies cry out for a restoration of traditional familial and social values; others call for new patterns of liberation. Third World peoples are angry at vestiges of imperialism and colonialism. People in a variety of national contexts suffer under totalitarian oppression. Economic and political programs—offered with revolutionary zeal and messianic fervor—have captured the imaginations of many.

Conflicts of this sort also cut through the heart of the worldwide Christian community. Antagonism is evident between rich and poor, East and West, North and South, left and right.

These conflicts, especially insofar as they contribute to the disunity of the body of Christ, are regrettable. The Christian gospel has clear political and economic implications, but it also stands in judgment on all human alliances, allegiances, and ideologies, particularly when they promote or manifest idolatrous trust. God's people in the present age have a difficult and complex calling. They must seek to promote the concerns and goals of Christ's kingdom in the flesh and blood realities of societal life. But they must also avoid the temptations that arise in the course of political and economic activity.

Many Western Christians have enjoyed the blessings of a social order that is committed to democratic values and a free-market economy. But we know that such a social order has its victims, at home and abroad. We must warn, therefore, against a myopic and self-interested celebration of our way of life.

Mindful of God's special concern for the poor and the oppressed, we must seek to promote laws, practices, and attitudes that will effect a more equitable and just distribution of the earth's bounty so that the hungry may be fed and the needy satisfied.

We hear with sympathy the contemporary cries for revolution against oppressive forces in our world. God's Word teaches that oppressive systems are condemned and that unjust rulers will be brought low by the only true and righteous Sovereign. God calls us to promote the good order and stability of the societies in which we live; to fulfill this calling properly we must refuse to obey disobedient authorities.

Recognizing these things, we cannot merely offer the counsel of patience to fellow human beings who suffer under the yoke of political or economic bondage. But on the authority of God's Word we warn against all forms of political and economic idolatry, whereby false hope is placed in the programs and promises which emerge out of a faith in human potential or the inevitable movement of history.

The human community today is beset by two opposing threats: a rampant individualism on the one hand and a totalitarian collectivism on the other. God's people must discern clearly the dangers posed by each of these forces. Individualism constitutes a clear denial of the covenantal bonds which ought to hold us in community with our neighbors and our God. Totalitarianism, whether of the left or of the right, attempts to impose a false community, conducting a frontal attack on the patterns whereby God ordered his creation. Both forces fail to respect the integrity of the family, the church, the school—and a variety of other institutions, associations, and spheres of activity which together are necessary to the fulfillment of our mandate. We call on Christians to oppose all forces—whether they are manifested in governments, corporations, or popular social movements—which seek to transgress or obliterate those boundaries.

(Previous synodical statements: Conscientious Objection and Tax Resistance, *Acts of Synod 1985*, pp. 463-73, 714-46.)

109. Who are some of the victims of our free-market economy? What does the Commentary mean when it says we must warn against a myopic and self-interested celebration of our way of life?

110. The Testimony says we are to work for the liberty of those who live under oppressive governments. How are we as ordinary citizens and church members to do this? Should we, for example, encourage our government to help overthrow an oppressive (but legitimate) government of, say, a Marxist-leaning country in Central America? Discuss this and other measures that we might take.

## MILITARISM, NUCLEAR WEAPONS

Following the Prince of Peace,
we are called to be peacemakers,
and to promote harmony and order.
We call on our governments to work for peace;
we deplore the arms race
and the horrors that we risk.
We call on all nations to limit their weapons
to those needed in the defense of justice and freedom.
We pledge to walk in ways of peace,
confessing that our world belongs to God;
he is our sure defense.

(Contemporary Testimony, 55)

Governments exist to provide order in societal life. In our fallen world they have been given the power of the sword to punish evildoers, to restrain sinful humanity, and to establish a just social order. Governments have this power for specific reasons; they may only use force and coercion to serve the goals of justice and peace.

Christians must submit themselves to all proper authorities. They must pray for those in authority, perform the good works which belong to citizenship, and—as fits with their callings—take part in the governing, policing, and defending of the nations in which God has placed them. They must carefully study governmental attitudes, policies, and actions, for Christians must obey governments only in those "things which are not repugnant to the Word of God" (Belgic Confession, Art. 36).

In the current political situation the phenomenon of militarism and the pattern of weapons development are of grave concern to the church.

We deplore militarism, in which a nation places its ultimate trust in its power to destroy enemies and boasts in its military might. Military programs are legitimate only when their purpose is to establish righteous relationships between nations and to deter international terrorism.

Since 1940 weapons of overwhelmingly destructive power have been developed. They are now deployed and stockpiled to serve as a deterrent to war. Because we hold to the "just war theory," which requires that the force used be proportionate to the goals pursued, we are convinced that this technology of mass destruction is incompatible with a just resolution of international conflict.

Therefore, we call on all nations, and especially on those in which we live, to halt the development of nuclear weaponry, to work hard for a ban on the manufacture and use of these weapons, and, with confidence in God, to accept the risks that are necessary to establish peaceful relations. And we call on Christians everywhere to pray and work for peace so that justice and peace may be visible internationally.

(Previous synodical statements: Statement on warfare, *Acts of Synod 1964*, pp. 85ff., 312-16; Guidelines re ethical decisions, *Acts of Synod 1977*, pp. 44-48, 550-74; Statements on war, *Acts of Synod 1982*, pp. 103-6, 615-21.)

111. How do you react to the strong stance of the Testimony and the Commentary against militarism and the continued development of nuclear weapons? Is it possible to condemn militarism without embracing pacifism?

112. Could nuclear war ever be a "just war"? Defend your answer.

113. What bearing should the prophecy in Isaiah 2:4 have on our attitude toward military policy today? May Christians assume that nuclear war is inevitable? Why or why not?

114. What are some specific ways that individual Christians can work for peace in our world, as the Testimony and Commentary call us to do?

## FUTUROLOGY, FATALISM, UTOPIA

Our hope for a new earth is not tied
to what humans can do,
for we believe that one day
every challenge to God's rule
and every resistance to his will shall be crushed.
Then his kingdom shall come fully,
and our Lord shall rule forever.

(Contemporary Testimony, 56)

We long for that day
when Jesus will return as triumphant king,
when the dead will be raised
and all people will stand before his judgment.
We face that day without fear,
for the Judge is our Savior.
Our daily lives of service aim for the moment

when the Son will present his people to the Father.
Then God will be shown to be true, holy, and gracious.
All who have been on the Lord's side
will be honored,
the fruit of even small acts of
obedience will be displayed;
but tyrants and oppressors,
heretics and all who deny the Lord
will be damned.

(Contemporary Testimony, 57)

Futurology studies the future. It should not be confused with eschatology, which studies the biblical message about Christ's return in the last days. Actually, neither study is only about the future. Futurology projects "possible futures" in the light of current trends. Eschatology talks about return, judgment, and the new heaven and earth in the light of the salvation achieved in Christ's life, death, and resurrection.

Futurology is done mainly on secular assumptions, which leave faith and God out of the picture. Projections of the future are made on the basis of measurable human decisions and "natural" developments. When chance and free decision are given a place in history, the future is seen as unpredictable. When predictability is desired, planning will try for total control, at the cost of human freedom. The optimist then predicts the perfect society, Utopia, as the result of careful planning. The pessimist predicts that society will destroy itself by the nuclear bomb, by using up all resources, or by pollution. The problem in such predictions is that they assume that either humans control the future, or it's up to fate or chance. Also, the optimist reduces evil to something that can be cured by education or social control. The pessimist accepts evil, all right, but places it in the structures of this world as something inherent.

A Christian view of the future must include human responsibility, the reality of evil, and the sovereign power of God in grace and in judgment. Human responsibility and God's rule are not a 50-50 proposition, each doing half. In the covenantal relationship human actions are a response to God and take place within his sovereign will. Obedience is blessed; disobedience brings judgment, now and in the future. This implies that we do not control the future, but at the same time it also implies that our responses make a real difference. For example, an economic depression may be understood as an act of God's sovereign judgment. Yet human beings are held responsible, in this case, for chasing the idol of economic growth and distorting the true meaning of life.

How should Christians face an uncertain, and even frightening, future? Is nuclear war inevitable? Or don't we need to fear complete destruction because "God would never let it happen"? Both the pessimist and the optimist here reduce humans to spectators. But Christian realism faces the threat of total destruction, confesses that God, who owns this world, will not allow that, and therefore does what it can to avert such disaster.

Christians do not look at the future with faith-less pessimism, nor with baseless optimism, but with hope-filled realism. Exactly because this is God's world, we must work for economic and social policies that respond obediently to God's call to live by his will in all of life. As we work obediently for a better future we cannot overlook the power of evil in human hearts. We must realize that no human planning can erase sin, and that no social policies can take away human responsibility. While working for social policies that are more obedient to God's will for human life, we must also call for personal repentance through faith in Jesus Christ. The combination of structural reform and personal repentance places the renewing power of God's salvation over against the deeply seated evil of our society.

Our serious efforts to renew our personal lives and to better our society must be suffused with longing for the return of Christ. His victory over sin and death will then be totally plain in the judgment on evil. The beginnings of his redemptive work that are found on earth will be purified and made part of the new heaven and earth, where righteousness is normal, and all tears will be wiped away. Then "the kingdom of the world" will be totally manifest as "the kingdom of our Lord and of his Christ, and he will reign for ever and ever" and we will reign with him (Rev. 11:15; 5:10; 22:5).

115. Is the fear of nuclear war pervasive in your life? Do you consider such a war likely in your lifetime? As a Christian realist, how have you learned to live with the threat of nuclear destruction? What, if anything, can an ordinary Christian citizen do to avert such a war?

116. According to the Commentary, our lives must be "suffused with the longing for the return of Christ." But do we really look forward to it? Does the biblical note of "Maranatha" ("Come, O Lord"; cf. 1 Cor. 16:22) ring in our hearts, echo from our lips, resound from our pulpits, arise from our daily routines? Was this forward-looking faith more real in other times? Would it make a difference if we were stripped of our affluence and comforts?

117. As we move along toward God's future, how are we to bring about a "combination of structural reform and personal repentance"? Must we choose between missions-evangelism and Christian social action? How are these two tasks related?

118. Share a passage of Scripture that you personally have found to be comforting and reassuring when looking to the future.